# ON DUTY WITH
# THE
# CHIEF

## PETER HAINING

EASTLAND POLICE

ANGLIA
Television Entertainment

BⱵXTREE

First published in Great Britain in 1995
by Boxtree Limited

Text © Peter Haining/Anglia Television Entertainment 1995
Photographs © Anglia Television Entertainment 1995

1 3 5 7 9 10 8 6 4 2

Designed by Sarah Hall

Typeset by SX Composing Ltd, Rayleigh, Essex
Printed and bound in Bath by The Bath Press for

Boxtree Limited
Broadwall House
21 Broadwall
London SE1 9PL

A CIP catalogue entry for this book is available
from the British Library.

ISBN 1 85283 928 7

# ACKNOWLEDGEMENTS

Special thanks to the following for their
help in the writing of this book: Chris Pye,
David Fitzgerald, Sue Gresty, Brenda
Reid, Ruth Boswell, Jeffrey Caine, John
Alderson, John Davies, Sue Heard, Maggie
Allen, Leaf Wigzell, Gerry Wigzell, Naomi
Philipson, Sandra Powell, and not
forgetting the members of the cast and crew
who always made my days with them such a
pleasure, and, finally, the Chief himself,
Martin Shaw.

# CONTENTS

1  WHEN FICTION BECOMES FACT  5

2  A DAY IN THE LIFE  13

3  THE FORCE BEHIND THE CHIEF  22

4  STAFFORD'S PATCH  43

5  THE CHIEF'S PEOPLE: Part One  56

6  CADE'S COUNTRY  72

7  AIRBORN WITH THE CHIEF  88

8  THE CHIEF'S PEOPLE: Part Two  91

9  THE MEN FROM THE MINISTRY  109

10  THE CHIEF: AN EPISODE GUIDE  118

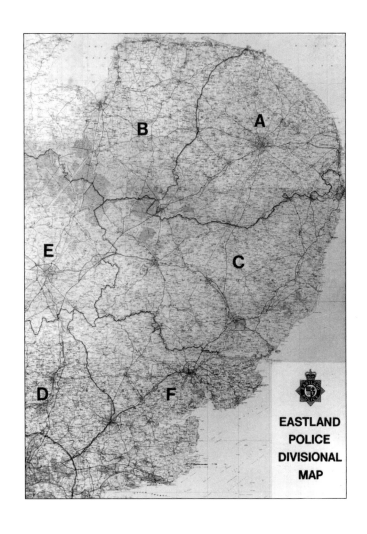

EASTLAND
POLICE
DIVISIONAL
MAP

# 1

# WHEN FICTION BECOMES FACT

'There's more to a chief than being a good detective.'

*THE CHIEF*
7 January 1994

This 'under-celebrated series which goes where no cop show has gone before' – to quote *The Sunday Times* of 4 March 1994 – which even its original creator and producer did not expect to last longer than six episodes, has now been on television for five years and become something of a legend for the uncanny prophecy of its stories about the latest developments in policing. Set in 'Eastland' – though there has never been any attempt to disguise the fact this is East Anglia – *The Chief* is, according to all the evidence, an extraordinary success story: a modestly budgeted drama series, the first to portray the higher echelons of policing, which has climbed from an initial audience of nine million to almost twelve million as the fifth series is transmitted.

Described at the outset as 'a mould-breaking drama' by *The Stage*, the paper the professionals read, it has been instrumental, too, in helping its stars, Tim Pigott-Smith, who played the first chief, John Stafford, and his successor, Martin Shaw, now appearing as Alan Cade, to largely subvert two of their earlier roles each has long wanted to put behind him. Both men have also made a little piece of television history by bringing to life men at the very pinnacle of the police force – two chief constables charged with keeping law and order in a sprawling corner of England and as ready to do battle with the local police authorities and Home Office officials forever frustrating their endeavours with new modes of bureaucracy, as they are determined to catch the villains and criminals who are supposed to be their primary targets. Uniquely, too, in no other series has the central character been re-cast with such ready audience acceptance.

*The Chief* can also claim a first in having a woman as an Assistant Chief Constable, Anne Stewart, played by Karen Archer, who the *Daily Star* quickly named, 'Britain's most glamorous Assistant Chief Constable'. Another more serious verdict of her role by the *Mail on Sunday* declared, 'The tension between her and the Chief is as constant and unpredictable as a

*The first Chief Constable of Eastland, John Stafford (Tim Pigott-Smith).*

love affair, which of course it can't turn into, which is certainly part of the fun.'

Anne Stewart has now herself been superseded by Detective Superintendent Rose Penfold, played by Gillian Bevan, who is also heading up the promotional ladder with the intention of becoming Cade's number two. The fact the series has had two top women police officers within striking distance of the Chief's chair is a nice acknowledgement to the real-life situation where there are now two women in this same position in the British police – a force for so long regarded as a totally male preserve . . .

The series is remarkable, too, in that it has won the approval of many police officers, not to mention being nominated for the Royal Television Society's RTS award for best drama series of 1990. In the news media at large it has been hailed as 'the most heart-warming cop offering since *Inspector Morse*' (Teresa Allan, *City Limits*) and 'one of the most ideologically interesting programmes on British television' (Lewis Jones, *Weekend Telegraph*). Nor has this success been confined entirely to the UK for the series is now also being shown in countries as far afield as Iceland and New Zealand, by way of Belgium, Holland, Israel, Turkey and even the Middle East. As Executive Producer Brenda Reid says with understandable pride:

'This is remarkable really, because *The Chief* is a very indigenous series and we run our police quite differently from everybody else. Yet we have had very good feedback from abroad – there are lots of people out there who just wouldn't miss it.'

The series has also been described as a programme that is actually helping the public to understand what is happening to the police. In the *Daily Mail* of 26 May 1990, the paper's Chief Crime Reporter, Peter Burden, wrote under a banner headline, WHAT THE CHIEF CAN TEACH US:

'At a time when public debate is raging around them, our police chiefs are constrained by rules and the nature of their job from giving their side of what appears to be an ever more disturbing story. But there *is* a way to see, at least at second hand, the problems which increasingly crowd in upon the country's fifty-four chief constables.

'*The Chief*, Anglia's drama series based on the work of a provincial police head, has struck such a chord with viewers. Fiction it may be, but it has given the public an unprecedented insight into the way a police force is run. If this remarkably successful series teaches us anything it is that local policing is critical in this country. Local police serve local people. And that is the direction we should follow for policing in the Nineties.'

Peter concluded his report, '*The Chief* shows that the only answer is to fight every inch of the way to prevent chief constables

*Eastland's current Chief, Alan Cade (Martin Shaw).*

becoming an endangered species. I'm afraid it's come to that.'

If the man from the *Mail* was afraid for the future of our top cops, he had no way of knowing that the future of the very series he had used to illustrate his argument had also for a time been under serious threat. For just as the most senior policemen had been battling with authority, so events were taking place behind the scenes at Anglia which could have halted the launching of the series. Indeed, the whole history of *The Chief* is dotted with incidents where fiction has foreshadowed facts, inciting both public and press concern.

Days before the first episode of *The Chief* about a prison riot was due for screening in April 1990, a real-life siege suddenly broke out at Strangeways. What John Stafford had faced in a reconstruction filmed months earlier in Glasgow's notorious Barlinnie Jail was now happening for real in London. It was a moment of crisis for the producer, Ruth Boswell, which she has never forgotten.

'It was an amazing coincidence that these troubles should have blown up just as the episode was about to go on air,' she recalls today, with the sort of smile that must have been very far removed from the way she felt then. 'There hadn't been a riot for years. Then the week we were due for transmission there *was* one! We had to be very careful, for although the film had been made some time before, we knew that some viewers might believe it had been made the day before and that we were somehow trying to cash in.'

In fact, the matter had to be referred to the Independent Broadcasting Authority, and while this was taking place the team who had just devoted eighteen months of their lives to bringing the series to the screen could only wait and hope. Would the TV watchdogs black out *The Chief* before it had even had a chance to get started?

'There was a very real possibility that the series would have had to be delayed,' Ruth says. 'But for how long no one could be sure. Fortunately after deliberating very carefully the IBA gave us the go-ahead. They agreed with us that although *The Chief* tries to reflect reality it *is* fiction.'

This bizarre coincidence undoubtedly intrigued far more of the series' first viewers than it annoyed – though few could have suspected it would prove to be the first of a number of similar incidents.

In April 1991, the second series opened with an episode about two policemen being blown up by a bomb – a story which mirrored what had just happened at London's Victoria Station when the IRA had planted an explosive. As in the previous case, the film had actually been made nine months earlier – a fact which the pre-screening publicity was at pains to point out.

Similarly during the second series an episode about toxic waste also foreshadowed a real incident. '*The Chief* must be psychic,' G R Kirk of Peterborough informed the *Daily Star* on 18 May 1991, 'after he investigated toxic waste being washed up on the Norfolk coast we had poisonous fluid washed ashore on the same coast.'

Then in January 1994 when Martin Shaw made his debut as the new Chief coincidence once more got to work. In this story, an IRA litter-bin bomb went off in a busy shopping centre with tragic results, leaving the police to argue with the anti-terrorist squad over the best way to deal with the outrage. The parallels between this fiction and the explosion of the litter-bin bomb in Warrington which had killed Jonathan Ball and Tim Parry were immediately apparent: yet here again the story had been made months earlier.

Nevertheless, a Warrington viewer, Mrs Eileen Heesom complained about the similarity to the *Daily Mirror*. 'To many of us in Warrington, it is still very fresh in our minds,' she wrote, 'Anglia TV phone lines were jammed the night *The Chief* was screened yet not one comment appeared in the press.' In fact, Ruth Boswell had already gone on record in a statement to newspapers emphasizing, 'The storyline was developed long before, and the case is really about the conflict between the police and MI5 and the action they take against an IRA unit.'

Since then, Anglia have also successfully defended the programme against complaints of violence, a lack of impartiality when dealing with the subject of abortion, and, on a somewhat smaller scale, distress to infants used in filming! A letter in April 1994 to *TV Times* from a Mrs E Brown of Bristol complained, 'When will producers stop using young babies in dramas where we often see them very distressed? In *The Chief* a baby was crying as the screen parents shouted at each other over its head. This must have had a terrible effect on the infant. Please stop these practices and think of the children.'

Ruth Boswell was, as ever, the calming influence. 'We used twins to make sure they weren't tired,' she explained, shedding a little more light into the complexities of film-making. 'At no time were the babies made to cry. Their mother was there at all times during filming. The babies cried when their mum handed them over for the scenes, but we felt they weren't in real distress.'

Such instances apart, few voices have been raised against *The Chief*, the quality of its scripts or the standard of acting.

'The writing is sharp, the pace is relentless and the searching treatment of police politics has added a new dimension to an overworked genre,' was *The Times*' verdict in April 1991; while exactly three years later in April 1994 after an extensive change of personnel *The Independent* was happy to refer to the programme as, 'an already fine cop series about the force's internal workings which crackles with new vigour.'

There have been some similarly interesting comments made about the two encumbants in the top job.

Tim Pigott-Smith was early on in his occupancy described as 'the cop with a conscience' (*The Stage*), 'an aggressive maverick' (*Daily Mail*) and 'the velvet fist in the iron glove' (*City Limits*). And in a later episode, his tough, outspoken and energetic personality also earned him a memorable – and much repeated – quote from some members of the Metropolitan Police Force he was investigating on charges of corruption: 'What's Eastland famous for? Sugar-beet. What do they call Stafford? Robocop!'

Martin Shaw, on the other hand, has proved a very different figurehead. *Today* called him, 'Mr Principles, a confident and first-class policeman'; while the *East Anglian Daily Times* (Eastlands' own) said he 'simply oozed charismatic maturity.' Other reviewers on the national press have added to the adjectives, referring to his Chief as, 'a high-flyer', 'street-wise', 'a suave dandy', and even 'a radical, controversial, one-man task force.' One thing they are all agreed upon, though, is that Cade is 'more unconventional and dangerous than Stafford.'

Not every viewer, however, has agreed on the relative merits of the two Chiefs. Both actors have their admirers and although

comparisons are sometimes invidious, two views should suffice to represent many more in demonstrating just *how* the series has built up its following.

'I used to wait excitedly to see the tall, smart figure of Tim Pigott-Smith striding along at the start of each episode,' Mrs K Collins of Gravesend wrote to the *Daily Mirror* in January 1994. 'He gave us a sense of pride in our police force, even though it was only acting.'

Northern viewer Mr L N Sandringham of Leeds had similar praise for his successor in the *Yorkshire Evening Post* later that same month. 'If all Chief Constables were as caring and involved as Martin Shaw, no force should be without one,' he wrote. 'My image was always of a pompous, aloof, overweight chief who was anchored to a desk. But in Alan Cade, Shaw brings a new dimension: attractive, menacing, penetrating, prepared to go to the heart of crime and corruption. Arguably, he is not the norm, but at the time of strained police-public relations, this series could restore needed confidence.'

If there is a secret to the success of *The Chief* aside from the quality of the acting and the production values, it has been the constant search for new ideas for its themes and storylines. This quest to be up with the new, even ahead of it, was the objective of the first producer, Ruth Boswell, and is now being pursued with equal dedication by her successor, John Davies, who has taken over the helm for the fifth series.

As the Executive Producer, Brenda Reid, who has been with the programme all along, puts it: 'I think we have succeeded so far by producing good, contemporary stories without ever losing sight of the integrity of the basic idea. That is our constant challenge.

'Mind you,' she told me during one of our meetings to discuss how the programme had begun, 'every series, when we are discussing possible new storylines, someone will always come up with the idea of doing "A Day in the life of the Chief" as being good drama. And every series I have to stop them from doing it because it would really be just a story of him driving about preparing a speech. The great drama would be: Does he get to finish writing the speech and deliver it?'

Her words stuck in my mind. If a day in the Chief's life was not something that could be shown on TV, I wondered, then why not in a book? It seemed to me an ideal way of starting to discover how the series progressed from script to finished episode. It would also enable me to begin discovering how the programme had originated, where the idea came from and meet the men and women who have been responsible for this latest TV crime drama success story . . .

*One of the many dramatic stunts featured in* The Chief: *a simulated explosion, filmed in Norwich.*

| | |
|---|---|
| **FULL NAME** | ALAN CADE |
| **BORN** | 10 JANUARY 1946 |
| **FATHER** | RAF WARRANT OFFICER |
| **PLACE OF BIRTH** | RAF BASE, WEST GERMANY |
| **EDUCATION** | DULWICH COLLEGE (Boards) |
| **QUALIFICATIONS** | Six O-levels (English, German, Maths, Geography, Art, English Literature) |

One A-level (English)
LLB (II.II) as a mature student –
University of London

---

### METROPOLITAN POLICE

**20 Oct 1963**  Cadet – Hendon Metropolitan Police, Cadet Corps. Middle-weight 'catch as catch can' wrestling champion. Gained A-level in Legal Studies. House Captain. 'A well-conducted, enthusiastic cadet who showed some leadership qualities. At times gave the impression of being withdrawn, or possibly more of a private person than superficial observation would indicate.'

**3 Nov 1965**  Police Constable on probation – West End Central Police Station

**4 Nov 1967**  Confirmed as Police Constable. 'Diligent and industrious. Shows much promise as an active ambitious officer.'

**8 Dec 1967**  Posted to Brixton Police Station. 'An active, well-conducted officer, who displayed a keen interest in criminal investigation.'

**1 Jan 1969**  Promoted to Detective Constable. 'An active officer with a good arrest rate.' COMMENDATION from his Commissioner for extreme determination and courage in bringing about the arrest of five drug dealers, two of whom were armed. He exposed himself to considerable danger in order to perform his duty.

**3 Jun 1971**  Promoted to Detective Sergeant and transferred to Chelsea. Selected for an Accelerated Promotion course at the Police Staff College, Bramshill.

**8 Aug 1973**  Promoted to Detective Inspector and posted to No. 9 Regional Crime Squad, New Scotland Yard. He showed a natural aptitude when dealing with organized crime. He began to develop a special expertise and knowledge concerning the international drugs trade, and an ability to co-operate effectively with foreign police forces.

**10 Sep 1975**  Promoted to Detective Chief Inspector and transferred to No. 2 Area (East End) – Area Major Investigation Pool.

**5 July 1978**  Promoted to Detective Superintendent to SOI Branch – International and Organized Crime Drugs Task Force. Visited Columbia, Mexico and the USA. Has friends in the FBI and the Drugs Enforcement Agency.

**7 Jan 1980**  Attends the Intermediate Command Course, Police Staff College, Bramshill.

**6 Apr 1984**  Promoted to Detective Chief Superintendent to remain in SOI Branch.

**3 Oct 1987**  Promoted to Commander in Command of SOI and is selected to attend the Senior Command Course at the Police Staff College, Bramshill. He is given special responsibility to develop international criminal intelligence and travels widely.

**3 May 1990**  Appointed Deputy Assistant Commissioner in overall command of Operations forces within his Specialist Operations Department.

**1 Apr 1992 -present**  Applies for and is appointed Chief Constable of Eastland, after much heart-searching and overcoming many doubts.

# 2

# A DAY IN THE LIFE

The Call Sheet indicated it was going to be a busy day for all those
working on *The Chief*. The three-page document issued the
previous night by the Unit Production Manager, Ted Williams,
listed the artists on call, the names of the camera, sound and
lighting crew members required for filming, plus a variety of
support personnel from a production runner to an entire catering
staff: a total of 86 people who would spend the day in studios not
far from Anglia's headquarters in Norwich.

The centrepiece of the huge operation which is required to
produce the episodes of the series is a cavernous building close to
the River Wensum at Mountergate, a short distance from the
city's famous Castle Museum. 'The Old Brewery', as the complex
is known (it previously belonged to Watneys, the brewers), houses
the sets of the various rooms in Eastland Police HQ: the Chief
Constable's office and those of his assistant and secretary, the
Conference Room, Control Room, Operations (Gold Command)
Room and the various other facilities for the senior members of
Cade's team. All of these authentic constructions, though nothing
more than skilfully crafted façades of wood and scaffolding, are
linked by a warren of corridors and passageways through which
snake miles of cable wires linking the powerful lights, sound
monitors and vision on-screens to the various positions where the
production team set up to shoot each scene.

Around these sets – which ostensibly make up the HQ of the
force at Pemberton Lane, Norwich – are draped huge backclothes
on which appear a photographic impression of the landscape all
around the building. But it is not a vista of Norwich or even
anywhere in Norfolk, come to that. For this panorama is, in fact,
the skyline around the Essex Police Headquarters at Chelmsford,
which, right from the start of the series, has been the real-life
location for all exterior shots of Eastland's headquarters. Here,
as with everything else concerned in the making of the
programme, no detail has been left to chance – even if the outside

world is only to be glimpsed for a moment through the blinds of an office window.

At the farthest end of the building from these sets are parked several 'action cars', the vehicles used on location as police cars, complete with their Eastland badges; and nearby the container of props which, among other things, holds almost 200 police uniforms. Both the uniforms and the cars have to be kept under strict security guard at all times because, as Ted Williams explains, they could cause a lot of trouble if they fell into the wrong hands. Indeed, Ted has had to provide the numbers of all these vehicles to the local police – but still recalls with a wry smile the occasion when one of the associate producers was driving one and was actually pulled up by a suspicious police officer!

The members of the technical staff are the first to arrive and begin lighting two sets – the Control Room and the Conference Room – which will be used for a total of seven scenes during the day. They are followed by the sound engineers and camera crew. All are in good spirits. The previous day's shooting – on location at Stoke Holy Cross in Norwich – has resulted in a record-breaking fifteen minutes of edited television time.

Producer John Davies, who is also an early arrival on the set, explains the sense of satisfaction this has given everyone: 'Shooting seven minutes of action in a day is normally reckoned to be a pretty good rate for television. Fifteen minutes must be some kind of record for a drama series like this.'

But John has only a few minutes to enjoy this achievement before the realities of filming to a very tight schedule break the spell. The lighting on the set suddenly goes out. The language which erupts, a mixture of the unrepeatable and the kind of resigned exasperation to this sort of occurrence that can beset any television production, echoes all over the huge building.

It transpires that because of the late finish the previous day, there has been little enough time to check over all the equipment before setting it up again this morning. And now someone has spotted that one of the generators which back up the huge supply of electricity needed to power all the equipment is leaking diesel fuel all over the warehouse floor. Fortunately, the trouble is quickly diagnosed – an air lock in the fuel system – and the lights are soon back on again. It will prove the first, though not the last, hiccup of the day.

The next principal to arrive is Rick Stroud who is directing episodes two, three and seven of the fifth series. A thick-set, energetic man with tousled blond hair, he carries about him the weight of authority of a director who has worked on television drama for many years. Starting at Granada, he subsequently worked extensively for LWT and earned a BAFTA nomination for

*The press releases distributed during two crucial press conferences for Alan Cade. Such attention to detail heightens the sense of realism in* The Chief.

# RELEASE

## EASTLAND CONSTABULARY

Eastland Police,
Police Headquarters,
Pemberton Lane,
Norwich,
NR17 5LO

Telephone No.
0603 768514

Date as Postmark

Subject:-     DEATH OF R

Unfortunately fol

last night withou

deepest sympathi

sense of shock

dnagers of rac

We are contir

stances of t

an Assistan

brought in

Headquart

t

Land

This is

that th

accusation which

the case is brought to the right cond

s

ious

that

triotic

but

Right su

again, we are still invo

his direction of the crime drama, *The Good Doctor Adams* which starred Timothy West. *The Chief* is his first assignment for Anglia.

Episode Three by Anthony Read which Rick is shooting today is yet another highly topical story about racial violence which erupts during a by-election in Eastland. The skinhead supporters of an extreme right-wing candidate, Walter Stone (Tim Meats) have become embroiled in a fight with some young Asians after a political rally. Although two of Cade's men sent to keep a watch on the meeting intervene in the fracas, one of the Asians, Rajiv Patel (Sandeep Kumar Rajput) is left unconscious and covered with blood. Almost at once both Stone and the leader of the Asian community in Eastland, Mani Shankar (Ayub Khan-Din), begin inferring that it was not any of their men who hit Patel – but one of the police officers.

All of this drama is to occur on a day when, according to the script, Cade should be meeting some representatives of the Police Federation and preparing a speech for a lunch the next day at the Chamber of Commerce. But any suggestion that we might be about to see a contradiction to Brenda Reid's edict is quickly dispelled . . .

The scenes to be filmed will show the news of the fight being reported to the Eastland Control Room followed by two crucial press conferences. At the first of these, Cade announces he has set up an enquiry headed by one of his senior officers to investigate the incident and, in particular, the complaints against his men. At the second, the truth about the allegations will be dramatically revealed.

Because of the particular demands of TV series-making, these three scenes which occur virtually at the beginning, middle and end of the story have to be shot back-to-back in one sequence of filming. This, naturally, puts special demands on the three actors most directly involved: Martin Shaw; Bosco Hogan, playing Cade's new Deputy Chief Constable, Wes Morton; and Gillian Bevan, as Detective Superintendent Rose Penfold, who is the other newcomer to the series.

The Control Room set is almost ready for action when Martin Shaw arrives at the Old Brewery. After exchanging a few words of greeting with some members of the production team, he heads for the make-up trailer to exchange the casual clothes he normally wears day-to-day for the impressive uniform of a Chief Constable.

Martin's arrival generates a sense of anticipation and excitement throughout the whole assembled unit. A believer in the maxim that a happy production team makes for better television, he has worked hard from the day he accepted the role of Alan Cade to establish a rapport with everyone associated with the series. His

mood all will tell you quite readily, helps to set the light-hearted, pleasant but always hard-working atmosphere that has typified the entire production on almost every day, even when the schedule has been at its tightest.

The transformation when he reappears from make-up is remarkable. Gone are the jeans and sweater and in their place a plain, white shirt, dark tie and neatly-pressed, blue uniform with silver buttons and a row of commendations which adds the weight of authority to his undoubted personal magnetism as an actor. All that is missing is the traditional police chief's hat, but Martin has steadfastly refused to wear one. It is not hard to see why this man has made Alan Cade, the radical policeman with a fierce integrity and devotion to duty, one of the top cops on the box.

Martin finds time for a few more words to other members of the crew as he makes his way across the warehouse to the set of the Control Room. He is obviously pleased when told the news about the previous day's filming. Then as he waits for the final checks to be made to the lights, camera and sound, he casually glances at some maps of East Anglia spread out on a table amidst the banks of computers and telephones in the nerve centre of Eastland HQ. They obviously catch his interest and he takes off the half-glasses that Cade invariably wears when reading or looking at documents.

'These are fantastic,' he enthuses to a production assistant.

*Martin Shaw on the set of* The Chief, *with his role model, Peter Ryan, the Chief Constable of Norfolk.*

'Where did they come from? They'd be wonderful for flying. They're much better than the maps I have.'

When he is not working, Martin's great passion is flying his own light aircraft and he is always happy to talk about the subject. As flying is also a hobby I have pursued myself for some years, it proved a common interest and one which we talked about each time we met.

After a rehearsal, Martin and Brian Bovell, who plays Cade's driver, PC Charlie Webb, briskly shoot the scene in which news of the fight is received. Then everyone moves to the adjoining set of the Conference Room where Cade will talk to the press about the inter-racial fight and be cross-examined by a journalist, Annie Miller (played by Jayne Mackenzie), who directly accuses him of operating a policy of discrimination against coloured people in the region.

I am invited to sit in while Martin, Jayne and Gillian Bevan – who Cade has put in charge of the enquiry into the actions of the two officers – rehearse their lines. As a former journalist in Eastland myself (West Essex, actually!), I was impressed all over again with the attention to detail lavished on the conference – even to the extent of preparing a press release on Eastland stationary complete with a photograph of Rajiv Patel, a copy of which was given to every reporter. All of this despite the fact the releases were scarcely visible to the camera and certainly not close enough to be read!

As I sit looking at one of these statements, Gillian Bevan appears on the set and joins Martin who is already seated behind a table facing the as-yet unoccupied rows of chairs for the journalists. She is a slim, attractive brunette whose varied career in the theatre and on TV has enabled her to bring a steely, highly professional edge to her characterization of DS Penfold – though not at the expense of her femininity.

Although Rose is a high-ranking officer in Cade's team as the head of CID, she does not wear a uniform. Instead she is dressed in a well-cut outfit of dark jacket and slacks which stylishly combine fashion with the authority of her position. Gillian smiles at Martin as she sits down beside him and is clearly a woman relishing her role in the series.

'I certainly am enjoying working on *The Chief*,' she tells me with one of her ready and engaging smiles. 'I'm a fan of Martin's like most of the female population!'

The scene is rehearsed by the trio and once Rick Stroud is happy with the result, the other extras who are to play the reporters, photographers and TV cameramen join the run-through. However, at the first take with everyone in their positions, Jayne Mackenzie fluffs her lines.

'Then why are you covering up for black troublemakers?' she stands up and demands of Cade. 'Aren't you in danger of losing the faith . . . '

Jayne stops, screws up her face and swears under her breath. She has obviously dried up.

Martin immediately grins up at her from behind the table. 'That's easy for you to say!'

The whole set, including Jayne, dissolve into laughter. Martin has once again deftly avoided any tension developing. Gerry Wigzell, the 1st Assistant Director and the man responsible for co-ordinating everything for the director, grins as widely as anyone. It makes his job of settling the cast down for a second take that much easier.

'OK. Let's go again. Nice and quiet please. We're rolling . . . Stand by and . . . Action.'

Jayne Mackenzie does not miss a beat this time. ' . . . Aren't you in danger of losing the faith of the men and women of the Eastland police force by being soft on them?'

The second take is perfect – and once again Cade, for all his maverick nature, handles the journalists' questions with consummate professionalism, refusing to be drawn on who might have attacked the Asian youth and fends off the accusation he could be instigating a cover-up.

'If it was one of my men,' he says, his dark eyes looking directly over his half-glasses into the camera, 'he will be rooted out and dealt with. The investigation will be carried out without fear or favour.'

Rick Stroud calls out 'Cut!' and then jokes aloud, 'One more blow for Fearless Jack Cade, the terror of the Filth!' – before sending everyone off, still laughing, for the lunch break.

The afternoon and early evening are to be concentrated on the climactic scenes in the Conference Room when the facts about what really happened during the fight are revealed. Once again the series' quest for authenticity is underlined by the fact that the dozen journalists and TV personnel who appeared at the earlier conference are now replaced by a new group of extras, the '1500 hour walk-ons', as the Call Sheet refers to them. Just as in real-life it would be stretching credulity too far to expect the press corps to be identical at both of these conferences, so a total of 38 local actors have found themselves with an extra day's work.

At this point, the series' other new co-star, Bosco Hogan, who is playing DCC Wes Morton, joins his colleagues on the set. A wirey, rather sombre-looking man in a uniform as immaculate as that of his boss, Bosco is a very versatile actor from Dublin with a typically Irish sense of humour. On camera, however, his clipped voice betrays not the slightest trace of his natural accent, while his

*Constantly in the public eye, Cade arrives for a press conference in the story called 'Old Scores'.*

restrained, very correct performance indicates that Morton is a rather traditional police officer not altogether at ease with his Chief.

'Actually, I've never played a policeman before,' he confesses, 'but because the people here have done such a lot of good research, there is always someone around to put you right if you stray a bit.'

Although Bosco has no lines to speak today, he is on camera the whole time and needs to display the necessary gravitas as Cade reports the death of Rajiv Patel, and then show surprise at the revelation of the police involvement in the young Asian's death. The scene itself is split into two parts. Firstly, Cade's announcement which is interrupted mid-way by a message brought in by a young policewoman that there has been a dramatic new development that requires him to leave the room for a few minutes. And, secondly, his return with the news of that development.

Martin's powerful delivery of the second speech holds the other members of the cast and crew in total silence throughout the rehearsal. It somehow seems to epitomize the Chief and all that he stands for . . .

'I am sure you all realize that police officers are often forced to tread a very narrow line in the execution of their duties,' he says, his eyes sweeping around the crowded room. 'In this case, that has resulted in a tragedy which everyone regrets, and no one more so than myself. But I would remind you that the tragedy could very easily have been the other way round, and that one of my officers was recently murdered in the course of his duties.

'However, that is no excuse for criminal acts, or even for offences against our own internal code of discipline. As Chief Constable, I have a very special duty to reassure the public. I also have a duty to reassure my officers that they will get fair play, and nothing more. They know that there is always a price to pay for justice and the rule of law. And as police officers, they are prepared to pay it.'

For the first time in the day, Martin actually stumbles over his line when referring to the police officer who had been murdered. He shrugs his shoulders and grins wryly over the top of his glasses at Rick Stroud. It has, after all, already been a taxing day – as have so many others during the making of the new series.

'OK. Let's take it again,' the director says, understandingly. 'From the lines, "But I would remind you . . ."'

Standing outside the set watching the scene on a monitor, I was suddenly struck at that moment by a strange coincidence. I had actually been on the location shoot when the murder of that policeman had been filmed. It now seemed a long time ago (although it was, in fact, only a matter of weeks), and in the interim I had not only found out how the series had been created, but met the team of people responsible for this and also learned about the previous actors who had helped launch it so successfully on the screen.

Indeed, as the shoot finished in Norwich that evening, and the cast and crew dispersed at the end of another almost twelve-hour day, my thoughts were once again drifting back to the days I had spent uncovering the origins of the programme in Herefordshire, Devon, London and Chelmsford, Essex where, five years ago, the basic concept had finally started to become a reality.

Like all the very best ideas, *The Chief* came into existence in the simplest of ways . . .

# 3

# THE FORCE BEHIND
# THE CHIEF

The idea for *The Chief* began as just four lines of notes that
scriptwriter Jeffrey Caine jotted down in a moment of inspiration –
and then 'put on the back burner,' as he describes it, until a
fortuitous phone call to his home in 1989.

Jeffrey, a former college lecturer turned novelist and now a
much-in-demand writer of television and film scripts, had made the
notes while ruminating on the one area of police activities he had
never seen on the screen.

'It occurred to me that with the proliferation of police series,
we'd seen a lot of canteen culture but nothing that focused on the
top end of policing,' he reminisced at his home in the picturesque
little village of Wilton close to Ross-on-Wye in Herefordshire. 'In
particular the problems that face the man at the top, balancing all
the influences and pressures that are on him from above and
laterally.

'I had this picture of a Chief Constable beleaguered by a
Thatcherite-like government and squeezed by a Thatcherite-type
Home Office. A man of liberal principles with a radical approach
to his job. It seemed to me that within this concept there were an
interesting set of problems that would make for a good series.'

Jeffrey had already, in fact, some experience of what made good
– and bad – television series. In 1985 he had written scripts for
*CATS Eyes*, a series for TVS about three female sleuths whose
activities were being secretly directed by the Home Office, which
starred Jill Gascoine, Leslie Ash and Rosalyn Landor. This had
been followed with some episodes for *Dempsey and Makepeace*,
LWT's series about the partnership of an English policewoman,
Makepeace (Glynis Barber) and a New York cop, Dempsey
(Michael Brandon) on reluctant attachment in London; plus work
for the BBC's long-running series about the Jersey detective,
*Bergerac*, starring John Nettles. Interestingly, the first two series
for independent television, *CATS Eyes* and *Dempsey and
Makepeace* shared the common feature of having been filmed

within their maker's own region: a factor that was to prove crucial, too, in the story of *The Chief* . . .

Like many a practised and imaginative scriptwriter in the television industry, Jeffrey is consulted from time to time by producers on the lookout for a new series.

'Actually, the idea of *The Chief* was first discussed with the BBC,' he reveals with a quiet chuckle at an old memory, 'but they weren't interested. Instead the Beeb went for another police series called *Waterfront Beat* about a bunch of Liverpool cops which flopped. I now think they rather wish they hadn't.' (*Waterfront Beat*, which starred John Ashton as a whizz-kid cop, Detective Chief Superintendent Don Henderson, who was forever in conflict with his major adversary, Superintendent Peter Fallows (Rupert Frazer), was said by its creator Phil Redmond – of *Brookside* and *Grange Hill* fame – to be about the 'personal and office problems of policemen.' It ran for just two rather disjointed and unsuccessful series in 1990-1.)

Jeffrey says that after this rejection he might well have forgotten all about the idea if his phone had not rung one morning in 1989 while he was working. On the other end of the line was Ruth Boswell, a freelance television producer he knew well. They had worked together before and shared a mutual admiration for each other's work. Their last involvement, however, had been in trying to set up an idea for a series which had also been turned down by – yes, you've guessed it – the BBC.

'The idea Ruth and I had worked on was about a female minicab driver,' Jeffrey explains. 'But the BBC didn't like that either. It was subsequently done, but astonishingly badly. Anyhow, Ruth said Anglia were looking for an idea for a locally-based series. Had I got any ideas? I couldn't think of anything else at that moment but *The Chief*, so once again I outlined my notes to her. She listened to me and when I finished she said just one word, "Terrific!" '

When Anglia also shared this enthusiasm for the idea of a show about a maverick police chief, Jeffrey was faced with expanding the four lines of notes into an outline for the TV company.

'Right from the start, the archetype of the Chief in my mind was John Alderson, the former high profile Chief Constable of Devon and Cornwall,' he says. 'Although I had no close connection with the police before I wrote *The Chief*, I knew we would have to form a really good association with them to make the series work, especially from the point of view of accuracy which would be vital if we were going to convince the viewers that what they were seeing really *could* happen. I also wanted the programme to have something to say, to be politically strong. I did not want it to be just another action or entertainment series.'

*Former Chief
Constable, John
Alderson, police
adviser to* The Chief, *was a constant source
of inspiration to Tim
Pigott-Smith.*

Ruth Boswell, an attractive and energetic lady with years of
television experience behind her, who lives in a spacious and
delightfully furnished Victorian house in the Muswell Hill district
of London, confirms that this is precisely what attracted her to
Jeffrey's concept.

'Jeffrey's idea was quite simple: "The Life of a Chief
Constable",' she says, 'but what really caught my interest was the
idea of him being a radical Chief Constable in the mould of John
Alderson. Jeffrey wanted to give an insight into decision making at
the very top level of the police. The other element that was so
intriguing to me was the fact that Chief Constables are the most
powerful individuals in the country, because nobody (she pauses
and repeats the word), *nobody* can alter their decisions unless they
are found to have been dishonest, corrupt or guilty of some similar
misdemeanour. They have responsibilities towards various civil
authorities, the Home Office and the people in whom they are in
charge, of course, but by tradition they are kings in their own
bailiwick. And that's what made the whole idea so exciting.'

Jeffrey Caine was, however, well aware that there was one
problem probably more crucial than all the others that would have
to be overcome right from the outset.

'The job of a Chief Constable is actually very boring,' he says.
'Most of the time he has to sit in his office, holding meetings,

moving paper, all that sort of thing. He is not normally in the middle of the action. Looking back, then, without the help of John Alderson himself there would have been no John Stafford. He proved to us it was possible to have a character like Stafford heading a Constabulary.'

These words are echoed by Ruth Boswell who also approached the series with no knowledge of the workings of the police force. A former script editor at ATV, a producer of children's programmes for Thames Television and then for eight years an employee of the BBC in their script and serials department (where she produced *Maybury*, the series about a psychiatric hospital starring Patrick Stewart), Ruth knew from the beginning that an immense amount of research would be required to make the programme authentic.

'The first thing Jeffrey and I did was to write to John Alderson,' she says. 'He immediately invited us down to his home in Devon and we spent a day with him. It was love at first sight for all three of us. We knew we were on the same wavelength. John is the most wonderful man – he joined in the project straight away with enormous enthusiasm.'

Jeffrey Caine takes up the story again: 'John understood exactly what I had in mind. He launched into a whole mass of stories about things he had done or things that he knew had happened to other Chief Constables. Initially he gave us a lot of storylines based on his own experiences, and once I was writing the scripts he was always happy to pass his comments on them. He was heavily involved in every episode right from the word go.

'Looking back, one of the nicest things for me has been the fact that we know people in the higher echelons of the police have watched the series and enjoyed it. I believe we have also demonstrated that a lot of people out there do enjoy an intelligent, well-researched police series which is not all action and has something to say about the politics of policing.'

Jeffrey – like Ruth Boswell – is happy to admit to the surprise both have felt over the extraordinary success of *The Chief*.

'When we started we thought what we had was a BBC 2-type serial that would run for about six episodes and that would be that,' the creator of the show now admits candidly. 'But even though it went out at a far from ideal time, it got these astonishing viewing figures and then one series became a second.

'Of course, after a while I felt the strain of having to produce so many episodes. I also had the urge to move on and do other things. It is very important for a series like *The Chief* to have a constant flow of new ideas, not to mention the introduction of new characters to enlarge the world of the chief and reveal more about his personality.

*A bird's-eye view, known as a cherry picker shot, of a demonstration against the dangers of BSE or 'mad cow disease'.*

'I think one of the hallmarks of *The Chief* has been its uncanny ability to predict events before they happen. I still smile about that very first episode in which I orchestrated a prison riot well in advance of the one at Strangeways! And we were on to the highly controversial subject of BSE – Mad Cow Disease – long before it became a topic of general discussion, too. There is no doubt in my mind that we opened up a whole new area in television drama as far as the police are concerned.'

The 'other things' which have taken up Jeffrey's time since he left the team producing *The Chief* have included a movie of his novel, *The Cold Run*, with George Siegel and Amanda Hayes; the script for *Heathcliffe*, the film sequel to Emily Bronte's classic novel, *Wuthering Heights*; and most prestigious of all the screenplay for the new James Bond movie, *Goldeneye*, the first to star the latest 007, Pierce Brosnan.

Like Jeffrey, John Alderson, who now lives in retirement near Exeter in Devon, clearly remembers the visit of the two guiding lights behind *The Chief* which has subsequently involved him in five unbroken years of association with the series. His enthusiasm for the concept has not waned in the slightest since that day.

'Yes, the vibes were definitely right, what the lawyers would call *ad edem*,' John says in the same measured and distinctive tones which were so familiar during his much publicized years in the police force. 'I have always enjoyed fictionalized drama on television and Jeffrey and Ruth's idea immediately appealed to me. The general public then had no idea of what goes on behind closed doors in the life of a Chief Constable: the internecine warfare, the battles with government bureaucracy, all that sort of thing. It was something I knew had never been done before and I very much wanted to be part of it.'

For several hours that summer day the two visitors listened while John, a raconteur of no mean skill, reminisced about his 36 years' experience as a police officer. He told them of important cases he had been personally involved with and recounted equally fascinating tales of the day-to-day minutiae in the life of a high profile chief. He reminisced about some of his contemporaries, too: all of them men operating in a world where law and order was constantly being subjected to new boundaries and guidelines.

When the writer and producer outlined to him the profile they were beginning to build up of their fictional chief he was both flattered and surprised.

'Initially, they were planning to call him Fielding,' John says, 'and he was a man very much like me. But I gather that when Anglia saw the outline their reaction was, "This man should be more of a bastard!" So although I would agree there were elements of me in John Stafford's character – he believed in the same things as I did – I would certainly not have run my force the way he did.

'Stafford was conceived as an idiosyncratic and aggressive policeman,' he goes on. 'But I always believed there were other ways of getting a job done rather than with aggression. You do have to be ruthless from time to time, of course, because there are tough decisions to be made. But in the final analysis Stafford's ways were not mine. However, I did strongly support the principles for which he stood, and the message he put across certainly illustrated areas of police affairs that were not normally covered by drama programmes.'

John Alderson also liked the idea of the series seeking to do what he considers good investigative journalism can do: 'Revealing to the public as much as it can, having regard to realism and to the undercurrent of police affairs and the power struggles that go on.'

And thanks to his unique experience as a 'hands-on' Chief Constable, he was able to give the series another of its guiding principles.

'It should not be a matter with every story of whether it has happened or not,' he emphasized to Jeffrey and Ruth then and repeats today, 'but *might* it, *could* it? Often there have been stories based on my own past experiences – like my refusal to arrest protesters at the CEGB demonstration – but on other occasions we have been very much looking in to the future.

'What has also kept my interest high is the fact that the series is being produced at a time when police reform is taking place across the board,' he continues. '*The Chief* deals with things that are changing all the time and we have had to get our facts right all along. I have always believed it has been an important part of my role to suggest storylines to keep the series up to date – and sometimes to even be ahead of events.'

John offered another important piece of advice to Jeffrey and Ruth at their first meeting. 'One thing I knew they had to avoid was creating a kind of detective series and sticking *The Chief* into it. I know a lot of scriptwriters love writing whodunnits, but the world of the Chief Constable is nothing like that at all.'

There were two other material items that he offered to his visitors in order to assist their research – copies of his authoritative and invaluable books, *Policing Freedom* and *Law and Disorder*, which are now listed in the pages of a substantial file, *The Chief – Bible*, which has been compiled by the Anglia production team as a guide to the series for newcomers on the writing, technical and performing sides. Apart from a section devoted to the 'Role of the Chief Constable' and detailed profiles of both Stafford and Cade, the *Bible* contains a wealth of facts and figures about police organizations, radio call signs, the running characters in the stories and the myriad other details associated with a series that now has its own complex history to which writers and performers must remain faithful unless they are to incur the anger of regular viewers.

Today, as the programme begins its fifth series, John believes that one of its greatest achievements has been to 'throw some light into the dark corners' of policing at the top.

'Even the average policeman doesn't know what goes on there,' he says, emphasizing each word. 'And in turn, Chief Constables have problems in keeping in touch with their men. I used all sorts of means to try and keep the members of my force informed about what was going on – by talking to their wives, by using the media, and so on.

'The series also portrays in fiction many of the dilemmas facing modern policing – and I believe that is helpful in promoting a better understanding of the terrific pressures our police are under. It has also addressed some of the issues of policing which impinge on the political system and that is certainly a unique feature among police dramas. *The Chief* has even been able to prove its diversity by switching from major international problems to many

*Stafford, revealing the aggressive side of his nature, in an angry scene with DCC Arthur Quine (Tony Caunter).*

of the domestic issues which every police force like the one in Eastland has to deal with.'

The resulting popularity of the series has understandably delighted John Alderson. 'I think television often underestimates the intelligence of its audiences. They are much more sophisticated than many people in the industry realize. Viewers have a real desire for knowledge and information about the police. Of course, there must be plenty of action and suspense in the series, but it is also entertaining and informative.'

John always grins wryly at newspaper reports that *The Chief* is 'the cop show the cops themselves like to watch'. Officers he knows have certainly given it full marks for detail, he agrees, and adds: 'They find it very topical and like the fact that the programme deals with the wheeling and dealing.

'A number of my former colleagues have taken me up on some things that have appeared in *The Chief* and I have found myself defending it. But generally I have felt quite comfortable with the storylines and been happy to justify them.'

Ever since the day Tim Pigott-Smith was cast as the first Chief, John has been in regular contact with him and his successor, Martin Shaw. Only the day before we talked he had been in London at the first rehearsal, or 'read-through', of the fifth series, offering his comments and advice to Martin and the others.

'Actually, being a Chief Constable is a bit like being on the stage,' he laughs. 'You have to get up in front of the public – but know what you are doing. I enjoyed working with Tim and now Martin because like the best actors they brief themselves very thoroughly on the parts they are playing. They both went to see Chief Constables in action and formed their own opinions quite separately from mine.'

Although John was undeniably the archetype for Stafford, Cade is, he says, wholly the creation of one of Jeffrey Caine's successors as scriptwriter, Ray Jenkins.

'This has resulted in two very different men. Tim was a hands-on Chief, outspoken and vigorous, while Martin is more inscrutable, deep and difficult to fathom. Of course, this has a lot to do with their backgrounds: Stafford coming from provincial Nottinghamshire, while Cade, the Met/CID man, is a much more cagey and political animal.'

Despite the many hours of discussion and consultation that John has put into the series over the years – some of it quite heated, he admits – it is still the very first episode with its prison riot storyline that remains his most enduring memory.

'It may have been because I had used similar tactics myself at Dartmoor in 1978,' he confesses, 'but it was just stunning to see everything on the screen. I remember thinking to myself as the credits came up, "Yes, it's really got it".'

Long before this initial broadcast, however, there was a great deal more work that Ruth Boswell had to do in convincing Anglia to invest the necessary £3 million to bring *The Chief* to the nation's TV screens.

'Jeffrey and I really went deeply into the working of the higher echelons of the police before we took the idea to Graham Macdonald, Anglia's Chief Executive,' she recalls. 'He liked it and commissioned a couple of trial scripts, but before we got the final OK we still had to do a lot of rewriting and a lot more legwork. But that was when we really set the style of the series.'

It was also at this point that an important fourth member of the team responsible for the creation of *The Chief*, came on to the scene. She was another widely experienced television producer, Brenda Reid, who would become the series' executive producer.

Brenda, who oversees the making of *The Chief* from her office in Anglia's London headquarters overlooking Leicester Square, is a woman of quiet authority hard-won as a result of years of making TV dramas. She cut her teeth as a script editor at the BBC with the much admired producer Innes Lloyd. Then after involvement with the hugely successful Alan Bennett season, *Objects of Affection*, in 1982, she became the initiator and producer of a series of single dramas by new writers entitled *Screenplay*. This

*An idyllic location in Cambridge forms the background to a meeting between Stafford and his predecessor as Chief Constable of Eastland, Terence Ogilvy (John Woodvine). Ogilvy warns Stafford against incurring the wrath of the authorities.*

she followed by producing two popular series at Pebble Mill: *Final Run*, about the IRA, and *Lizzie's Pictures*, a poignant story of a woman reaching the age of 40 and restarting her life. Brenda was brought to Anglia by Graham Macdonald with a brief to run the drama department and seek out productions that could be made with the studios and production staff already available at the Norwich-based company.

'It was a challenge that I relished,' Brenda says, gazing out of her large picture windows on to the bustle of London below, 'because there is a lot more pressure on a commercial company to deliver popular entertainment. When I saw the outline for *The Chief* it seemed to me that it fitted the ITV brief for popular drama. I was also looking for ideas that came at subjects from different angles, that represented a different perspective. I didn't want to do just another straight police show.

'*The Chief* seemed very much like a chance to do a police series with a difference. Not a day-to-day cop show, but one about the power and the politics that govern the police. How the power is used and operated – that seemed to me the most exciting thing about it. A popular drama series – but one with something to say. Nobody had looked at the police in this way before so we decided, "Let's go for it".'

As Executive Producer, Brenda's job is to give the initial go-ahead to a storyline and then offer her opinions on the first and subsequent drafts of a script. Though the actual running of the series is in the hands of the producer, her overview and now exhaustive knowledge of the history and development of the series which she has been able to pursue without being subjected to the day-to-day pressures of film-making, is invaluable.

Brenda emphasizes once more the importance of John Alderson's involvement in the ultimate success of *The Chief*.

'John is a remarkable man,' she says. 'He was the only one who stood up and gave evidence at the Scarman enquiry. He was well-known as a liberal and for that reason a slightly dangerous, edgy Chief Constable. As a founder member of Charter 88, he stands to the left of centre, rather than to the right of centre. That made him an unusual man in the Force – and a perfect collaborator for the series. He put Ruth and Jeffrey in touch with a lot of people in the police and his input has been terrific.

'He's been a wonderful source of ideas, too. When we meet, he'll say, "Did you see that story in the paper about such-and-such – well, that reminds me of a Chief Constable who . . . " and off he'd go. In my opinion it is his series. He *is* the Chief!'

But just like Jeffrey Caine and Ruth Boswell, Brenda was not blind to some of the inherent problems in their concept.

'We realized right from the start what the difficulties as well as the pluses were going to be,' she continues. 'The difficulties being that, in truth, a Chief Constable spends most of his time addressing lectures, attending important dinners, travelling around. He gets involved in the actual "dirty work" of crime very rarely. So when subsequently this has been levelled at us as a criticism – "A Chief Constable would never be involved on the streets in *that* way," we have been told on many occasions – we reply: "We're only seeing six or seven incidents in his life – depending on the number of episodes in any series – and we're picking the six or seven days in the year when something *does* happen!"

'Although accuracy is supreme,' she adds, 'it is also very, very important that we know exactly who is controlling who and where the decisions are being made.'

Brenda naturally shared the view of Jeffrey and Ruth that the series would be most effective set outside a Metropolitan area. East Anglia seemed to have everything to offer as a background and was therefore disguised with the thinnest of veils as Eastland.

'Anglia TV has a commitment to represent its region, of course,' Brenda explains. 'It is a lovely area and people do like to see the scenery. So we decided to try to represent it by shooting on location as much as possible. Shots of two people talking over a desk can be very boring. The concept also gave us a chance to represent some of the feelings in the area.'

Once Anglia had decided to give the go-ahead to making an initial series of six episodes of *The Chief*, the next vital decision was to cast the leading role.

Both ladies have slightly different memories of this event. Ruth Boswell believes that Graham Macdonald made the initial suggestion; Brenda Reid thinks the credit belongs to Ruth. What is beyond doubt is that they all agreed on Tim Pigott-Smith.

'We all felt he seemed absolutely right,' says Brenda. 'Apart from *Jewel in the Crown* he was not terribly well known as a leading TV actor. I don't think we even considered offering the role to anyone else.'

Ruth Boswell then made the initial approach to the actor. 'I contacted him when we had a first draft of the script,' she recalls, 'and he was politically very interested. It was also just the right time for him to take a lead in a television series. Tim committed himself to us from a very early stage.'

The series also needed a female lead and here the producer and her team decided to take a bold gamble and make her a policewoman of almost equal rank. Ruth explains this second crucial piece of casting.

'We were trying to anticipate what might happen in the police in terms of rank so we created Anne Stewart and made her an Acting Chief Constable which gave her the possibility of becoming a Chief Constable. It is also a much better rank than that of Deputy – which is more about administrative work – because an AAC is out in the open and in the action. So that's why we made Anne the ACC Crime.

'We also wanted to show a woman in a high position in the police because it is only lately that they are beginning to creep into the top ranks. We also decided to give her a lot of personal problems because being an ACC is a very demanding role for a woman with two children. We orchestrated the break-up of her marriage even though her husband had left his job to be with her. But he was unable to find work and it all became too much. One of the reasons why he couldn't find work was because he had been blacklisted by a local MP – which was based on a real instance. That was another example of *The Chief* using a true story in a fictional plot.

'The series has had several looks at prejudice against women in the police,' she adds. 'It has also focused on the dilemma many professional women encounter – how to juggle their working and private lives successfully.'

As the stories and cast were taking shape, Ruth Boswell next sought the assistance of the local police forces in East Anglia.

'Their response was marvellous,' she enthuses. 'We were offered unstinted and unlimited co-operation from all ranks without any questions being asked about how we were portraying them.'

She singles two men out for particular mention: Peter Ryan, the former Chief Constable of Norwich, and John Burrow of the Essex Police Force in Chelmsford.

Once shooting had begun on the first series in 'The Old Brewery' at Norwich and on location in Essex, Suffolk, Norfolk and even the outskirts of London, Ruth started talking up the programme which had now been in gestation for over a year.

'*The Chief* is different from any other police series,' she told her first press conference to announce its start of transmission in April 1990. 'It's about the politics of policing, the accountability of the police to a fast changing society. It's not about bobbies on the beat and car chases. It deals with the concepts of policing in modern Britain. We have tried to reflect reality in our storylines, and the series will be controversial. After all, any series about ideas and ethics is bound to be controversial.

She added, 'The series reflects current issues, their impact on the police, the dilemmas they create and the radical thinking necessary to resolve what are frequently contentious issues. Unlike any other police series, *The Chief* concentrates on the political manoeuvreing necessary to fulfil the demands of both the police and a budget-conscious government.'

When the first episode was finally transmitted, Ruth and the members of the team could only sit at home and wait for the verdict of others. Curiously, Brenda Reid experienced exactly the same kind of reaction that John Alderson had done.

'Of course, I always hoped it would do well,' she says, turning once again to look out over Leicester Square as she collects her memories. 'But it was only when I sat at home and watched the first episode on transmission as opposed to seeing it in its many, many earlier forms as I had been doing in the previous months, that I suddenly got a really good feeling about it. It was the first time I could look at it quite coldly and think, ''I believe we've got a hit.'' People had been saying to me that it could run, but it was at that moment I began to *believe* it. It's had the odd hiccup since then, but nothing really serious – and here we are on the fifth series.'

That first feeling Jeffrey Caine and Ruth Boswell had shared that the series would probably not go beyond one season was quickly dispelled with the news that it had attracted an average audience of 8.4 million viewers. When it was voted one of the most popular new television dramas of 1990, the idea of a second series was not just a possibility but a certainty.

Brenda Reid has now had time to examine the series and its

elements and what turned it from an unheralded and rather off-beat police series into a ratings winner.

'Interestingly enough, it is all the things I hoped it would be and none of the things I feared it might be,' she says. 'The one constant thing that people love about *The Chief* is its politics. The fact is it is about power, manipulation, control – all of those things. Now in those episodes where we need to vary the story and force the Chief into some tiny local issue we find those are the ones the audience don't like as well. But when he's out on the streets actually doing it . . . Bingo! It's really strange.

'What audiences also loved about it from the very beginning was the fact that they are seeing how the system works. Especially when the police are in the news the whole time, when they are having a very hard job and coming under a lot of criticism. *The Chief*, though, presents a very positive side, it makes it understandable how mistakes can happen, how people can get corrupted, who's pulling the strings – all of that. Viewers just love it when the Chief has a battle with the Home Office!'

Letters from these viewers expressing their opinions have poured into the production office ever since the series went on the air. They have been written by all age groups from teenagers to OAPs. Most have been very positive – although there have been some complaints, too.

Either Brenda or Ruth Boswell have made a point of responding to all of them.

'Accuracy has always been a key word in *The Chief*,' says Ruth. 'It's absolutely essential that we do our homework properly or somebody will find fault. In all the 28 hours of the series I was responsible for I don't think we ever got a serious detail wrong.'

Violence in the stories is, though, one issue that has produced heated reactions, as Brenda Reid explains.

'We had one complaint to the Independent Television Commission upheld against us for showing a gang of kids going into a shop holding a milk bottle full of petrol with a wick on it and threatening the shopkeeper. It was a story about vigilantes which posed the question, "Does a person have the right to take the law into their own hands?" After showing that episode we were accused that it could give rise to "copycat crimes". The complaint was upheld by the ITC which was possibly fair.

'There were also complaints about us showing the vigilantes taking off the main offender to a deserted warehouse. He was obviously terrified and when he got there they threw what he thought was petrol over him. It was actually water. Now I don't believe *that* was unnecessarily violent.'

Brenda has very strong views about violence on television.

*A police raid on a pub, where drug dealing was rife, developed into a violent affray in the first series of* The Chief.

'It's not that I am afraid of it or that I believe that it encourages violence,' she says. 'In fact, I believe that in dramatic terms the more you leave to people's imaginations, the more exciting it is. I always refer any scriptwriters to the scene in Roman Polanski's *Tess* where a horrendous murder has taken place in the upstairs rooms of a building. The camera takes you into the room below and you see a drop of blood fall from the ceiling, followed by another and another. You have no idea what has gone on upstairs – but, by God, it sends a chill straight through you.'

Brenda, who says she was introduced to drama listening to Saturday Night Theatre on BBC radio, believes the imagination can conjure up things far more terrifying than any film could do. 'I really don't want lingering shots of corpses and blood and all the rest. I'd much rather leave it to the imagination!'

Controversy, as anticipated, has also gone hand in glove with *The Chief* ever since that first episode about the prison riot. In the fourth series a story about an anti-abortion campaign spearheaded by a militant American produced quite a storm, too, says Brenda.

'I think it is immensely important to always try and strike a balance when you do a story about abortion,' she says. 'I don't believe it is interesting to see just one point of view. The main issue, though, was not for or against abortion – but people's right to choose. We actually didn't go out of our way to show the Home

Office in a particularly sympathetic light, for instance, so we couldn't be accused of balance there! Mind you, I don't think it is the job of drama always to be balanced – I think you are allowed to be biased.'

In fact, eleven complaints about the episode from viewers who felt the portrayal of the anti-abortionists lacked impartiality and was unfair to opponents of abortion, were rejected by the ITC.

'We also stirred some people up with a story about legalizing drugs,' says Brenda. 'That episode was actually done at my suggestion because I had read a report about a Chief Constable who had come out quite heavily in favour of de-criminalizing certain drugs. I said that this was exactly the sort of thing that Cade would do. In fact, it turned out that a lot of people felt it just wasn't believable.

'The interesting thing was they had forgotten the *facts*. That a top policeman had said that, and we had researched the subject very thoroughly. "Oh, no," we were told, "A Chief Constable wouldn't have the right to make that decision, it's the law of the land." I was sad that it was dismissed in that way.'

Ruth Boswell, for her part, remains surprised as well as understandably satisfied, about the number of times *The Chief* has been 'ahead of the game' with its storylines.

'It's been quite uncanny,' she says, 'we have found in nearly every series that something we created has then actually occurred. For example, we had an episode about a hoax bomb that wasn't followed up by the police. That was a storyline I literally made up over lunch one day in Leicester Square. And believe it or not, on the week we transmitted the episode there was the Victoria Railway Station bombing and the spate of hoax calls that crippled the country's rail links to London!'

Perhaps an even more extraordinary instance of *deüjaΥ vu* occurred when *The Chief* featured a story about BSE – 'Mad Cow Disease'. Ruth still finds the events difficult to believe today.

'If you remember, the draft of the Public Broadcasting Bill contained a clause in it at one stage which would allow any policeman to walk into a broadcasting station and impound a tape to stop it being transmitted. It followed on from the Duncan Campbell episode in Scotland – but fortunately the clause did not get into the final Bill. I started to wonder what the impact of such a clause would actually mean in real life . . .

'Then I remembered an idea I had tried to get on the BBC about BSE and thought of a way of combining the two in *The Chief*. So with this in mind we sent Stafford off to look at the Channel Tunnel and left his deputy in charge. At the same time a fictional broadcasting station in Norwich was making a radical documentary about BSE which linked Alzheimer's Disease with

Mad Cow Disease. In the story, a journalist warns one of the big-wig local farmers about the documentary and the harm it could do. The farmer goes straight to the deputy and threatens him into doing something about it. So the deputy sends some policemen off to the station to try and stop the documentary from being transmitted.

'Now, all this was taking place before the film had even been viewed, so what the farmer was attempting to do was exercise editorial control on a programme he hadn't even seen. We did a lot of research into BSE for the story, intending to make some very strong points about it – though I must stress the episode was not primarily about BSE but censorship.

'To cut a long story short, someone in the Ministry of Agriculture got to hear about our programme and there was enormous pressure brought to bear on the Anglia management. We were asked to alter the documentary. There was an absolute furore and in the end a compromise was reached. But the strangest thing of all was that at that moment in time we hadn't finished the script, nor had we shot the episode. Yet here we were getting editorial guidelines!

'What I still find so remarkable about the whole sequence of events was that a story we had invented about editorial control on something that hadn't been viewed was exactly what happened to us. It was such a mirror image, I can still hardly believe it.'

A problem of a rather different kind and one that neither Ruth or Brenda Reid had anticipated was having to replace their leading man when Tim Pigott-Smith decided to leave the series. But this proved to be the moment when the initial concept of *The Chief* came uniquely to their aid. For unlike any other show, they could replace one Chief Constable with another and hope for complete audience acceptance – as long as the new man was right, of course. Why, though, did their star decide to leave the series he had helped to make so popular?

'Quite simply, Tim didn't want to become typecast,' Ruth says. 'He felt he could be falling into a trap. He just didn't want to be in a position where he was doing series after series.'

Before making his decision to leave, however, Tim had made a plea for the Chief to become involved in European policing, Brenda Reid reveals.

'Tim had quite firm ideas about his character. He thought we were in danger of running out of steam unless we opened up the boundaries and went into Europe. Rightly or wrongly, we decided against it. We felt *The Chief* would instantly become a different kind of series.

'Certainly we have dabbled in Europe a bit throughout the series, but those episodes have always proved to be the most difficult. We just decided there was enough going on politically in this country as far as the police were concerned for us to be able to reflect all kinds of changes without the need to go to Brussels or wherever.'

Ruth Boswell also expands quite readily on this concept which never materialized.

'I think it is fair to say we always wanted a European dimension to *The Chief*, and I did give a lot of thought to the idea of doing a story in Europe. We even had a number of storylines up our sleeve which could have been used, but there would always have been a lot of practical problems to consider and in the end the economics defeated us.'

And so with Tim's decision to go irreversible, the production team decided to turn disadvantage to advantage by 'promoting' John Stafford to a job in Europol in order to explain his departure. There was, then, of course, the matter of creating a new Chief. Clearly there was no point in looking for another Stafford and so Ray Jenkins, now one of the regular members of the script team, was set the task.

Ruth Boswell picks up the story again. 'Obviously we didn't want someone to just step into Tim's shoes. He had to be a very different character played by a very different actor. Ray invented Cade almost exactly as you see him on the screen today.'

Armed with a profile of the new head of Eastland, the team next started looking for an actor to bring Alan Cade to life. 'We went through a very long list of names,' says Ruth, 'and auditioned quite a few people. But once Martin Shaw had been suggested he was absolutely the obvious choice.'

Brenda Reid also shared her enthusiasm for the commanding, handsome actor. 'Martin is such a charismatic actor – he is one of those performers who has matured and got better and better as he has got older. I don't think *The Professionals* stretched him very far. But in the interim I've seen him in various productions in the theatre and doing some interesting smaller things on TV – not a great deal of what I regarded as 'quality television'. From our point of view he could deliver an audience – he was very popular with viewers as well as being a good actor – and the minute we thought of him there was no one else in the running.'

Ruth Boswell was once again the member of the team who showed the initial script for the new Chief to Martin Shaw. He was immediately interested, she says, especially because he felt it was a good moment in his career to be playing a role that was both popular and serious.

Like his predecessor, Martin has also made personal contributions to the character of his Chief – not least in giving him the passion for flying which he himself shares – and at the same

*Stafford with his formidable PA Fiona, played by Erin Geraghty. She will be familiar to many viewers for her roles as a nurse in series such as Angels.*

time helping to boost the series' viewing figures to almost twelve million. He is now very much the Chief.

Ruth Boswell has herself decided to follow the lead of Jeffrey Caine and Tim Pigott-Smith and move on to develop other television projects – hoping that fortune might once again bring her another success story.

'I think I have achieved all I set out to do with *The Chief*,' she said as we finished our conversation in her home. 'You can get stale after a while and I thought the time was right for somebody else to come in and maybe do something different.'

Her own immediate plans are to film Shane Connaughton's novel, *The Run Of The Country*, for Channel 4 with Albert Finney in the leading role. Interestingly, Finney plays a stern police officer whose teenage son runs away from home . . .

'I will always have a soft spot for *The Chief* and watch it with interest,' she says. 'It's been a bigger success than any of us expected and as long as Anglia can keep finding the stories there's no reason why it shouldn't run on for years . . . '

Ruth's departure from *The Chief* naturally lead to some restructuring in the team working on the fifth series, with Chris Pye, Anglia's Chief Executive of Entertainment joining Brenda Reid as joint Executive Producer, and the experienced director/producer John Davies taking over the Producer's chair.

With the programme now so well established, the aim of this group has been to develop the appeal of the series further and thereby attract more viewers – an ambition both John Davies and the new script editor Maggie Allen are well equipped to fulfil.

John Davies came to *The Chief* fresh from working on two of the most successful and long-running crime series on independent television: the TVS series, *The Ruth Rendell Mysteries*, and Anglia's highly-acclaimed adaptations of P D James' stories about Commander Adam Dalgliesh, starring Roy Marsden. Prior to this, from 1964, he had been a drama director, probably best known for his TV versions of classic novels such as Emile Zola's *Germinal* (1967) and *Nana* (1968); *The Woodlanders* by Thomas Hardy (1970); and the BBC's expensive and reverent 20-part adaptation of *War and Peace* in 1972 with Anthony Hopkins, Rupert Davies and Faith Brook.

John branched into police series in 1985 as the director of the third Dalgliesh story, 'Cover Her Face' in which the Commander tracked down the killer of a drugs racketeer. He followed this with 'A Taste For Death', about some unpleasant anonymous letters which lead to a gruesome double murder (1988) and most recently 'Devices and Desires', the case of a psychopathic killer on the loose (1991). John actually orginated *The Ruth Rendell Mysteries*, taking the idea of a series based on the best-selling novelist's books to TVS who, 'bought the idea within half an hour' and signed him up as producer/director. The result was a stunning success when the very first episode of 'Wolf to the Slaughter' in 1987 got into the Top Ten ratings. Never one to stand still, however, John moved on to new projects at the end of the first series.

A tall, quietly spoken man who exudes professionalism, John sees his role on *The Chief*, modestly, as that of 'a jobbing producer just trying to ensure the continued success of the series.'

He had no misgivings, he says, when asked to take over from Ruth Boswell. 'I've been associated with Anglia for years while I was making the P D James series, so one naturally takes an interest in the other things they are doing. I actually remember when *The Chief* started and the production team moved into the offices next to mine. I watched what they were doing, but never dreamt that one day I would become involved.'

With the formula and central character already firmly in place, John's task is clear.

'We are going to try and find ways of reaching an even larger audience,' he says, 'but hopefully without blunting the edge of the political issues or any of the other elements about policing at the top that have made the series popular. Among the subjects we shall be tackling are the arming of the police; the rights of protest and civil liberties; attitudes towards race and gay and straight sex;

methods of dealing with young offenders; and police corruption. And all the time, Cade's continuing battle with the Establishment.'

John has had the added challenge of casting and introducing three new characters to the series: DCC Wes Morton, DS Rose Penfold, and Andrew Blake, the new man from the Ministry, played by the well-known actor, Julian Glover. Cade's interaction with all three will set the pattern for the seven episodes.

'The whole series is working towards a showdown between Cade and the Establishment,' John Davies says. 'The moment when they finally try to pull the rug from underneath him. For although Cade is an honourable, straight man, he will not compromise. And naturally this leads to the question: Will he or won't he go . . . '

Providing this major cliffhanger for *The Chief* on which the series's future will hinge, is primarily the job of Maggie Allen, the warm, chatty, red-headed new script editor. She, too, comes to the job with an enviable track record and a lifetime of experience of the police behind her. In fact, Maggie actually began her working life as a secretary in the police force in Plymouth and during her subsequent career in television has been associated with such famous series as the BBC's *Z-Cars* and Thames Television's long-running *Special Branch*.

'Over the years I have got to know a lot of people in the police force,' she says, 'and I pride myself on having a special knowledge of police procedures. This is very important on a show like *The Chief*, but I'm very glad to have the expertise of someone like John Alderson to call upon.'

Maggie, who has been working against a tight deadline to organize the scripts for the fifth series, took the unusual step of writing the first episode, 'One Of Our Own', about the police use of guns which has a tragic result for a member of the Eastland force. She is, in fact, the first woman to have produced a script for *The Chief*, a record which will not last long as she has commissioned another female writer, Susan Wilkins, to create a later episode, 'Drawing the Line'.

'A series like *The Chief* has to have a constant flow of up-to-the-minute ideas,' she says, 'which means new writers and that is very much my aim. I also want to get more excitement into the series, more action, and a generally quicker pace to the stories. Fewer faces talking over desks which can be very boring. This will not, though, be at the expense of the tough political edge which has made the programme so unique.'

I discovered all about the latest series when I went to a night shoot but first I learned all about the first three series of *The Chief* and its original star, Tim Pigott-Smith.

# 4

# STAFFORD'S PATCH

## For Eastland HQ Read Chelmsford

The county town of Chelmsford is located in the southern half of East Anglia: a kind of gateway from the overcrowded sprawl of London into the huge area of cultivated farmland and picturesque small towns and villages stretching from the Thames Estuary to the Wash which make up Essex, Suffolk, Norfolk and Cambridgeshire. Once a rural haven on the old coaching routes to Colchester, Ipswich and Norwich, the town is now bypassed by the busy A12 which runs all the way up to the North Sea coast as far as the port of Lowestoft and holiday resort of Great Yarmouth.

Although Chelmsford is still famous for its livestock market which began about AD1200 and is now acknowledged as one of the most important in East Anglia, the town itself has of necessity changed as a result of the demands of industry and today acts as home base to, among others, the Britvic soft drinks company whose illuminated clock on the outskirts is a familiar sight to all road and rail travellers, and Marconi, the communications giant.

It is, perhaps, appropriate that a series all about the high-tech of modern policing should have chosen for its fictitious head-quarters the town where the very first public broadcast took place. It was in a tiny factory in New Street, Chelmsford that the Wireless Telegraph & Signal Company transmitted its pioneer radio programme – a news bulletin – on 23 February 1920. The company, later to be known after its founder, Guglielmo Marconi, was responsible for introducing radio to the United Kingdom, but was almost at once stopped from transmitting by the Government which feared, apparently, that civilians were about to take over the ether to which the British Forces believed they had first rights! Two years later, however, the decision was reversed and Sir John Reith was charged with setting up the British Broadcasting Corporation. Ever since, Chelmsford's niche in the history of radio has not always been accorded its due, but a blue plaque has at last been placed on the wall of the factory in New Street.

*The maverick Chief, John Stafford, outside the Eastland 'headquarters' in Chelmsford, Essex.*

Aside from its 15th Century Cathedral, the 18th Century Shire Hall, and modern County Hall, the centre of Chelmsford is now wholly given over to a pedestrian roadway and shopping precincts. Less than a mile away in the attractively named Springfield area are the looming fortress of Chelmsford Jail on Sandford Road and, opposite, the Headquarters of the Essex Police Force. The prison itself has recently been refurbished and strengthened to cope with an increasing population of inmates; but the impressive group of two story, rich red brick buildings which comprise the county base of the Essex police force are still redolent of an earlier, more stylish age. With their tall, ornate chimneys, white-pointed facia, large windows and arched doorways, there is an undeniable air of stability and calm about the complex. A tarmacadam drive up to the front entrance which passes well-manicured lawns and a small copse of trees enhances the undeniable impression that this is an establishment devoted to law and order.

It certainly made an instant impression on Ruth Boswell when she was hunting for a suitable location for the headquarters of Eastland Police.

'We went out to Chelmsford and I was rather expecting one of those grey concrete blocks,' she recalls. 'Instead we drove into this beautiful Victorian building with "Chief Constable" written on the wall in brick. So even before I was properly introduced to the Chief Constable I said, "Can we use this?" '

Only the exterior of the building is ever seen in the series. By the magic of television, when the Chief walks through the front door at Chelmsford he emerges one hundred miles away in those offices especially built in, 'The Old Brewery'. Of course, great care is always taken in creating this sleight of hand – and so successful has it proved that a number of policemen working in the Essex HQ have been told insistently by local residents that they have seen them on TV during scenes of the Eastland Force in action!

Little change is actually needed to be made to the exterior of the Chelmsford HQ whenever the unit move in to film some scenes, usually on a Sunday. Work goes on in the building as if nothing untoward is happening outside – despite the generator lorries, cabling, cameras, crew and actors milling around the front area. The only really noticeable change is the large blue board complete with the familiar police symbol and the words, EASTLAND POLICE HEADQUARTERS, which is put up on the wall near the main entrance. That and the superb, plum-coloured, chauffeur-driven car with its tinted windows in which the Chief travels around his filmland patch.

It was on a summer day in 1989 that the man who was to become the first Chief of Eastland met the man who was actually the Chief of Essex Police Force and in so doing set in motion the whole saga. In fact, Tim Pigott-Smith retains an affection for both the locality and the policemen of East Anglia who helped him take on a role which at that time was unique in television history.

A slim, erect man in his late forties, with bony features, hard blue eyes and sparse blond hair, Tim has a naturally authoritarian manner which makes it easy to understand why he was such a natural to play a man like the Chief. Indeed, he became a household name as the 'policeman we loved to hate', the sadistic and corrupt military policeman, Captain Ronald Merrick who tortured an innocent prisoner for a confession of rape in Granada's acclaimed 1984 story of the last years of the British Raj in India, *The Jewel in the Crown*. The success of *The Chief* has, however, enabled him to a large extent to live down the reputation that series gave him, although there are still certain things about it that even now make him laugh.

*The Chief on the move, in an early episode of the drama.*

'To begin with, people would shout hatred at me in the street, but I just kept on smiling,' he recalls. 'I particularly remember one man standing next to me on the Tube. He looked up and recognized me. He just said, "Oh, bugger" and ran off – I never saw him again. The same thing happened in New York while the series was being shown. I went into a shop and the girl on the door almost had hysterics. "Oh, my God, it's him! The Thorn in the Stone," she screamed. Apparently *The Thorn Birds* was running at the time and so was the film *Romancing The Stone*. I don't quite know how she got them all into one title, though!

'I was also holidaying in Spain while *The Jewel in the Crown* was being shown on TV there. It had been re-recorded in Spanish and it was just hilarious to watch. The way they'd dubbed my voice, I became a real Mexican bandido. Afterwards I was known locally as "El Malo" – the baddie.'

Tim, who was born in Leicester, and now lives in a beautiful, double-fronted Edwardian house in Highgate, North London (appropriately just around the corner from the local police station!) had no such dreams of international stardom when he became interested in the theatre as a child. Indeed, he had a narrow escape from death when he was an infant which, he says, is one of the reasons he is an upbeat, irrepressible character in both his private and professional life.

'When I was about two years old I had an injection to clear up an abscess, but developed an allergy to it and went into a coma,' he says. 'I can vaguely remember coming round. I had irregular blood counts until I was about 16. I've tried not to look back since.'

The rest of his life has been on a more even keel, although there has never been much doubt about his ultimate destination. 'I went to Stratford first when I was ten,' he recalls, 'and then when I was eleven I saw Olivier as Coriolanus. At the age of sixteen, I actually moved to Stratford when my Dad became editor of the local paper, the *Stratford Journal*, and I was sent to Shakespeare's school. After studying English, Drama and French at Bristol University I went back to Stratford once again and joined the Royal Shakespeare Company.'

Tim soon proved himself a talented actor alongside a number of equally gifted contemporaries including Jeremy Irons and Simon Cadell. In the ensuing years he enjoyed playing a wide variety of stage roles – predominantly in the classics – and gained experience of television in, among other things, the love story, *Hannah*, playing the bank clerk, Mr. Blenkinsop; he was the scientist Francis Crick in *Life Story* which was voted best TV film of 1987; and then the ruthless Hamer Shawcross in *Fame Is The Spur*. But it was undoubtedly the one-armed villain Merrick who made him a household name, gave his bank account a considerable boost and allowed him to be selective in his choice of roles.

Tim had, though, no reservations about accepting the part of another policeman when the first scripts of *The Chief* were shown to him.

'Basically, I suppose, because Stafford was a nice policeman with two arms and no gun,' he reflects with a grin that is far removed from the snarl that made viewers shiver whenever Merrick appeared on their screens. 'Also, because the series was obviously going to be something very different. It was about an area of policing that had not been dealt with before on TV and with a format that would impart new information. The philosophy of the series also appealed to me, the notion that the police force is there to protect the welfare of the public. I thought, too, it would encourage people to ask themselves what they wanted out of the police; what their job should be and how much they should be under Government control.

'The only similarity between Merrick and Stafford was that they were both policemen,' he continues. 'For a start Stafford was a happily married man without any of Merrick's dark personal problems. Had Merrick been in Stafford's place, he would have emerged a dictatorial mini-Hitler. And although Stafford was tough, he was liberal minded and promoted the welfare society as well as arresting criminals who endangered it. He was very much a new-age policeman, believing in the force being accountable.'

Tim pauses and his eyebrows flex into the now-familiar V-shape which he has used throughout his career to express every strong emotion from anger to intimidation.

'Stafford was like me in that he always spoke his mind. Because I'm straightforward, I often give the impression of being blunt and sometimes rude. Yet I don't intend to be. I know it would probably be better if I chose subtler means of being honest, rather than telling someone I think they're an idiot, but that's just the way I am. I must admit I don't spend an awful lot of time organizing my behaviour to suit other people.

'Stafford didn't suffer fools gladly, either, and he came on pretty strong most of the time. He was dictated to by no one. But he was essentially an honourable man – a liberal who shot from the hip. A tough man who found himself drafted into an area with a sleepy force where the crime rate was rocketing and the arrest rate plummeting. He didn't like that at all, and while he was cleaning the town up he made himself very unpopular. But even though he was a first-class police chief, he wasn't able to cope with his own family so well and had trouble with both of his children.'

With his Shakespearian background, it is not surprising to find that Tim draws comparisons between Stafford and other roles with which he is familiar. It is only the role that is surprising: Brutus. Tim played the man who knifed Julius Caesar in a touring production just after completing the first series of *The Chief*.

'They both have a certain moral integrity,' he explains of this apparent dichotomy. 'Not many people understand their nobility because it's fairly dated in the modern world, but I think that the Romans and the British have an awful lot in common. When Shakespeare was writing, the Elizabethans saw themselves as latter-day Romans, holding the centre of a world stage. Those values lasted until World War II.'

Like the thoroughgoing professional actor he is, Tim went to great pains to research the role of a Chief Constable.

'I read a lot – the police are always issuing papers, the process of self-inquiry never stops – and shadowed the Chief Constable of Hampshire, John Hoddinott, for a day. Such a man is immensely powerful. It was fascinating to see how people reacted to that power, to see how much space they gave him to be what he wanted to be. The chief constables really are like God to their officers.

'It was the new breed of younger chiefs who really impressed me, though. Men like Geoffrey Dear in the West Midlands and Peter Ryan in Norfolk – they represent a wave of liberal academics. That was the sort of character I tried to create with Stafford – an idealist who knows that there are flaws in the system and tries to correct them.'

Tim pauses again as if reconsidering the names he has just mentioned.

'I suppose if you could put a career down on paper for Stafford, Geoffrey Dear would be nearest. Starts young, is picked up as a fast flier, pushed through quickly, sent to Bramshill, read law at university and gets a degree. Someone like Dear has had to go through every layer of policing in order to achieve the top level and has an understanding of what people are about.'

In fact, Stafford's personal file in the production team's Bible states that he was more a mixture of all the nation's select band of 43 chiefs than being based on any particular one – John Alderson notwithstanding! Like his real-life counterparts, he had come up through the ranks – each Chief Constable must touch on every rank, however briefly, on the way to the top – but was spotted early and sent first to the Police Staff College at Bramshill House in Hampshire and then to university to study law.

Having followed the same path as all the force's brightest recruits, Stafford then likewise emerged with their dislike of smug bureaucrats, a stern belief that rules were meant to be kept, and a deep seated respect for the law. All such men, Stafford included, may seem tough and unsympathetic, but they want to do their very best for the community.

The law was therefore Stafford's real standpoint, the file adds. He had to ask himself: Who am I answerable to? The Police Authority? The Home Office? And his answer was: The Law through Parliament. Knowledge of the Law must be absolutely paramount to the Chief, and Stafford saw it as his duty to put that law into practice in whichever way he considered best.

Returning to the actual presentation of his character on the screen, Tim draws another parellel to his favourite classics: 'In a way it was a bit like creating a king in Shakespeare. Leadership demands that you fill space. I know it's a clicheü to say so, but my opinion of the police as Dixons of Dock Green was destroyed by their activities during the miners' strike. The trouble is we only meet the frontline police who are under tremendous pressure. The men I met were hugely moral and motivated by goodness. They are people constantly trying to make things better, desperately trying to do a good job.

'Did you know the word police comes from the Greek *politeria* which means protection and welfare . . . What I liked about the scripts was that they showed you had to be tough to be liberal.'

It would be wrong, however, to imagine that Tim has nothing but praise for the police. He has had run-ins with the law, both as a private citizen and as a driver. (He is, incidentally, the owner of an immaculate MGB sports tourer which he drove a couple of times in the series.)

'My first encounter was with a traffic cop about twenty years ago,' he smiles. 'I was doing 45mph along London's Embankment when this policeman stopped me. When I asked why, he said, "Because I couldn't catch the bloke in front!" I have also met a couple of our older chief constables and they were sexist, racist, chauvinist pigs.

'I must also admit that like some of the other members of the cast who joined at the same time as me, I went into the series feeling a bit anti-police. Most people are. They think the police are tough and fascist-like and we all talk about how young the cops look these days. But the more policemen I met and the more I understood about what they had to face up to, the more my attitude towards them changed.'

Tim is also quick to pay tribute to John Alderson for helping him to change his viewpoint and in the creation of the role of Chief Constable Stafford.

'There was an element of John Alderson's liberality in Stafford. John always wanted to do things his own way. He refused to police secondary picketing during the miners' strike and he wouldn't issue his men with plastic bullets – those are very much the sort of attitudes Stafford had.

'In fact, John is an altogether remarkable man and I still think about him a lot,' Tim says, almost wistfully. 'He's a great analyst of what's going on in society and the world. I remember he told me one day, "You have to be tough to be liberal, Tim." On another occasion when we were talking I said to him, "Give me a scenario for nightmare policing in the 1990s." He said, "Okay, Waddington, the Home Secretary, is a hanging man. Thatcher's a hanger. There's a sudden terrific increase in violent crime, and under pressure of a Tory majority, capital punishment comes back. Then an 18-year-old Muslim shoots Salman Rushdie. Now that's international.'

Despite the variety of locations used during Tim's tour of duty as the Chief – ranging from Barking on the eastern fringe of London (for a drugs raid) to quiet, Norfolk fishing villages – it was the proximity of the Eastland HQ to Chelmsford Jail that served as an ever-present reminder of his dramatic introduction to the life of a Chief Constable when, in the very first story, he was called upon to quell a prison riot. Unfortunately, the local jail was too crowded to accommodate any filming and Anglia had to settle for the notorious Barlinnie Jail in Glasgow which was then being refurbished and had little space unoccupied by inmates. Tim recalls those first days as a hard-pressed top policeman very vividly.

'Barlinnie has the reputation of being one of Britain's most hardline prisons,' he says. 'In fact, three years before we went there, there had been that terrible explosion of violence when the prisoners rioted and held some of the officers hostage for five days. So I had to be smuggled into the jail wearing a raincoat over my uniform. In fact, we had to be escorted everywhere by prison officers, and for our own safety we were told to keep our uniforms covered up on our way to and from the set.

*Dramatic confrontation for Stafford in the first episode of* The Chief *which was filmed in Barlinnie Jail, Glasgow.*

'We actually filmed the scenes in a newly decorated wing which was still empty, but to get to it we had to walk through the main prison. If the prisoners had seen me in my uniform they would have rioted. They hate the police. I have to admit I have never been so scared in my life – the place was terrifying.'

The shoot took three days during which time Stafford – according to the script – was able to quell a riot without force by using a dose of good old-fashioned, no-nonsense talking. Interestingly, the parts of the rioting prisoners were actually played by some of the prison warders while they were off-duty.

'Apparently, the warders regularly take the part of rioters to train new recruits,' Tim says. 'Afterwards, one of them came up to me and said, "Well, I've got to admit it, Tim, I'm impressed." I thought that was a pretty good omen for me.'

The experience made a deep impression on Tim, too, and, a year later, during a break from filming *The Chief*, he voluntarily visited another prison as part of a theatrical tour promoting the plays of Shakespeare.

'I had this feeling that long-term prisoners were starved of any kind of culture,' he says, his voice measured with an emotion built on personal experience. 'Prisons are such depressing places. These recent disturbances just go to show that if you treat people like dirt they behave like dirt. Prison is totally degrading – even the loos just have stable doors – and there is no chance of retaining your dignity. That's why drama is so important – it can channel these energies and give people a sense of self-respect.

'In any event, when a colleague and I went on tour I made sure that several jails were on the itinerary. We started at Nottingham Prison and performed readings from *Julius Caesar*. Once again, I admit I was terrified. But it wasn't because I considered the prisoners a threat to our safety. Heaven knows what crimes they had committed, but they were as good as gold. I was just terrified of patronizing them, of appearing to talk down to them. And of course I had doubts about them enjoying Shakespeare. When we started, a few of them said, ''What a load of rubbish'' and that sort of thing. But many of them really enjoyed it.'

Such was the response to the tour, that Tim plans to go back inside again when a suitable opportunity arises. He feels playing one side of the law has helped give him a better understanding of those on the other side of it.

'I think it is partly a sense of guilt which makes me so keen,' he admits. 'As a society we ignore people who are shut away in jails for long periods of time, and such neglect is only storing up trouble for the future. A prisoner who has been locked away for years without any real contact with society has less chance of rehabilitating himself when he finally comes out.'

Recognition of a less unnerving and rather more pleasant sort was soon being accorded to Tim in the world at large when *The Chief* began transmission.

'When I was on tour after the first series the recognition I received in the street from people who had watched the programme was the same as I had when I played Merrick. Then a year later when I was in Cardiff one day I happened to be listening to a quiz on a local radio station in which listeners were asked which television programme made my name. Most people rang in to say *The Chief*. That was rather gratifying.

'I then started being asked to give speeches at police functions. I had to be very careful not to pontificate! There was also an extraordinary occasion when I was drawing some money from a cashpoint and I was saluted by a senior police officer who happened to be passing. He said how much he was enjoying the series!'

And an even more startling example of how convincing Tim had made his portrayal of Stafford occurred when he was filming a scene in London.

'I was sitting in my official car while we were filming. I was wearing my uniform, when all of a sudden this old lady came up, rapped on the window, and demanded that instead of sitting there

I get out and do something to sort out London's traffic problems!'

Another of Tim's favourite episodes from the first series saw him face trumped-up charges in a story that had shades of the John Stalker affair.

'It wasn't meant to be a drama documentary about John Stalker as some people wanted to suggest,' he says, 'but the programme did raise some of the same issues. It was all about a man who would not see the law compromised in the interests of national security. I read John Stalker's book as part of my preparation and now I do sympathize with anyone whose career is founded on principles.'

Was he surprised at the almost immediate success that the series enjoyed?

'I didn't think it would be so popular,' he says with the same frankness as Jeffrey Caine and Ruth Boswell. 'I mean who knew what a Chief Constable was? When I was a boy we used to see the Chief Constable driven around in a big, black limousine. I thought he was some kind of judge. The series certainly opened my eyes to the really amazing jobs senior policemen do. Sure there are a few rotten apples, but most of the coppers I met do an absolutely fantastic job.'

The lessons which Tim learned from playing the Chief in the first series inspired him to make some changes in the second. He deliberately made the character a little less abrasive and perhaps a bit more diplomatic.

'In the second series, Stafford came back like a boxer who had gone in very high and been floored by the end of the first round,' he reflects. 'His idea of the autonomous chief ruling his own patch had been seriously undermined and he was horrified by the political machinations that went on, not to mention the pressures that were placed upon him.

'He was a bit disillusioned, in fact. His morality, idealism and determination were intact, but he was now prepared to be more cautious, to play the game slightly differently in order to get what he wanted. Whereas in the first series he would go crusading into a situation, in the second I endeavoured to portray a man who was controlling himself more, being more political and recognizing realities.'

Tim was also pleased at the way issues raised by the series were drawing comment from both the press and public – and how a number of the stories had proved uncannily prophetic.

'It was really interesting watching the way other people's attitudes changed while we were making the series. They felt that the police were a necessary evil. But gradually one realized that they are seriously motivated and very moral men. I'm very much in favour of raising public awareness of issues – it is the

fundamental value of television. It is a voice, so use it.

'And although the incidents in the stories were fictional, we seemed to have anticipated a number of events. In fact, nearly everything that happens in *The Chief* was taken from something in real life. It just goes to show how people like John Alderson, Ruth Boswell and Jeffrey Caine have their finger on the pulse.'

Much as Tim says he enjoyed playing *The Chief*, his heart still lay in the theatre – and in particular with The Compass Company, an acting group founded in 1984 by Sir Anthony Quayle and dedicated to taking good plays to the regions. On his death in 1989, Sir Anthony had bequeathed the company to Tim, but the actor's commitments with the Anglia series had made it impossible for him to do anything about it until the following year. Then, in March 1991, he announced he would not be continuing as the Chief beyond the opening episodes of the third series, after which he intended to run Compass as the actor-manager. He also, he said, hoped to be able to spend more time with his lovely, red-haired wife, Pamela, who is an actress (and has appeared with him in productions for The Compass Company as well as in TV productions like the BBC's *Morphine and Dolly Mixtures* in which she played a schoolteacher who befriends an abused girl) and his teenage son, Tom.

*Stafford, with his second in command, Assistant Chief Constable Anne Stewart (Karen Archer), on the hunt for a marauding gunman.*

'I've loved my time in *The Chief* and I am a total supporter of the series and its aims,' he told a press conference. 'It's simply that I don't want to play a policeman any longer. As Stafford I've spent more time in a uniform than most Chief Constables because it works better dramatically. But I get fed up being behind a desk and having to wear a restrictive uniform – it limits people's views of what you are capable of. *The Chief* has been my longest-running part since Merrick and I'm proud of the acclaim that has been given to the series. But now it is time to do something else.'

Tim was understandably worried about being typecast and having to carry the burden of Stafford around with him for years as he had earlier done with Merrick.

'We've done two extremely good series,' he added to the press, 'but I've been typecast before and I feel I have done everything with the character I can do.'

However, this bald statement disguised behind-the-scenes attempts by the production team of *The Chief* to get Tim to continue in the now very popular role he had created from nothing. He was, he admits, tempted to go on – but only if Anglia had allowed him to take *The Chief* into Europe.

'I think the problem is that the character has definite limits,' he says 'and there was no point squeezing the orange until it is bone dry. Perhaps if the series had moved out of Eastland and into the wider area of Euro-policing there would have been more scope.

'For some time I have said I would like to see more of the European connection on television. Through an intelligent drama series people could pick up a lot about what is going on in Europe. I think viewers learned a lot about the work of a Chief Constable through *The Chief* – I know I did. So in the final analysis you can say I would have been interested in playing Stafford again if a new series had included stories about Europe.'

What Tim did agree to do was to appear as the Chief going into Europe as the head of Europol in Brussels, while his successor, Martin Shaw, was introduced as his replacement.

'The Brussels job was good for Stafford,' Tim says of the character he made flesh and blood for millions of watchers before disappearing from view. 'If the real-life rumours that the number of constabularies are to be halved, from around 43 to 25 – which were rife while I was filming *The Chief* – are true then Stafford would have fought it like mad. And he would have had an increasingly bad relationship with the Home Office.'

Having played his final scenes, Tim then took to the road with The Compass Company's major revival of Peter Shaffer's *Amadeus*, playing Salieri. Once again he was able to draw parallels between his former role as a Chief Constable and his new job as an actor-manager.

*A rare moment of tranquility for the Chief and his wife, Dr Elizabeth Stafford, played by Judy Loe. The MGB is Tim Pigott-Smith's own car.*

'Both of them have to motivate the people they are in charge of. And for that you have to have a clear vision of what you want to achieve. My ambition is to get the company up and running and established and then when I think it is strong enough, to move on. I am at a time in my life when I ought to be doing all sorts of things. The danger is that I will miss opportunities by continuing to work with Compass for too long.'

Sadly, *Amadeus* proved the company's last touring production when vital financing broke down. Though naturally deeply disappointed, the ever-resilient Tim immediately turned to new projects – including a possible return to the world of crime as a North London private eye, Duggan, in an idea he has been developing with Desmond Davies, one of the directors on the second series of *The Chief*.

There is also one other rather more unusual ambition he nurses. For, the man who has brought a new meaning to the word Chief Constable in a portrayal that mixed authority with an unbending morality, would actually like to appear in non-other than a sit-com.

'I'd love to do something completely different from *The Jewel in the Crown* and *The Chief*,' he smiles in the friendly and relaxing manner so different from his usual steely television roles. 'A sit-com would be nice. Although whether my face would allow it is quite another matter . . . '

# 5

# THE CHIEF'S PEOPLE: Part One

## Series 1-3

### THE RESILIENT PARTNER

#### Dr. Elizabeth Stafford (Judy Loe)

The beautiful, auburn-haired actress Judy Loe who played Chief Constable John Stafford's GP wife, Elizabeth, brought a special insight to her role as a professional counsellor that was drawn from her own personal suffering. For apart from losing both her parents when she was still a child, her first husband, the actor Richard Beckinsale, co-star with Ronnie Barker in *Porridge*, died of a heart attack at the tragically early age of 31. Judy had also suffered from recurring back pain for many years, and while appearing in *The Chief* caught a mystery bug that she feared might be the so-called 'Yuppie Flue', *Myalgic Encephalomyelitis* or M.E.

Judy's experiences have not, though, made her either bitter of withdrawn. Indeed, she still flashes an enchanting smile using her striking green eyes and laughs engagingly when talking about the positive aspects of her life. She can even make a joke about the fact that in recent years she seems to have been cast rather often as a policeman's wife.

'I was pretty well and truly into what I called my "Copper Phase" when I was working on *The Chief*,' she recalls, 'On the one hand I was Tim Pigott-Smith's doctor wife, and at the same time I was in *Eurocops* on Channel 4 in which I was a policeman's widow romantically involved with detective John Benfield.'

There were, though, great differences between the two roles.

'In *Eurocops* I was the love interest,' Judy says, 'but in *The Chief* I had to be the supportive wife, mother and professional woman all rolled into one. Stafford had to rely a lot on Elizabeth's objectivity and support to do his job. And she in turn needed to be very resilient to be able to combine her busy life as a doctor with equally hectic domestic commitments. And as if that wasn't enough there were the problems with the two children!'

Resilience is very much a word that summarizes the roles that Judy Loe has been called upon to play in her career as well as her private life.

Born in Urmston, Manchester in 1947, her childhood ambition was to be a ballet dancer and she went to Birmingham University where she gained a BA in English and Drama. But tragedy had already impinged on her life, and the square set of her jaw reflects the inner strength she needed to face up to these traumas. The same inner strength which she utilized to make Dr Elizabeth Stafford a strong character who was so popular with viewers – especially women.

'I was only eleven when my mother died and my father had to look after me,' she says wistfully. 'Then I lost him and it was very hard indeed for me. Ever since then there's been a great need in me to be needed, to serve people. I suppose I am a bit of a chameleon, which is not a bad thing for an actress. I tend to be what people require of me, or what I think they require of me.'

Judy turned this quality, not to mention her looks and her talent, to good use when she went on to the stage and appeared in a variety of productions including *Hair, The World of J.B. Priestly* and *No Sex, Please, We're British*. On television she had an early taste of police life in *Z-Cars* and *Crown Court*, followed by *The Upchat Line, Robin's Nest, When The Boat Comes In* and *Life After Death*.

Her marriage to the comedy star Richard Beckinsale brought her joy and tragedy in equal measure. She gave birth to their daughter, Kate; and then in 1979, her young husband collapsed and died while filming *Porridge*. For a long time after that there was no other man in her life and she admits she was looking only for friendship.

'It's very hard for someone who's been in a relationship, whatever the end has been, suddenly not to have the intimacy, based on history, relaxation and security with someone,' she confides.

Judy was still in the process of coming to terms with Richard's death when she met Roy Battersby who directed her in the ITV comedy series, *The Home Front*, in which she co-starred with Brenda Bruce and Warren Clarke. Despite an eleven-year age difference, they discovered a mutual attraction and have been a couple ever since. Roy also became her director on *Eurocops*.

'Making *Eurocops* with him sort of tied everything up beautifully for us,' says Judy. 'It was the first time we'd worked together since we met and being with him like that brought home to me everything I love and admire about him. I have my own identity now. Actually, I never was the "tragic widow" figure that I was made out to be in the press. I've always been a coper.'

In 1989, Judy needed to be able to cope when her career suffered something of a setback. For the first half of that year she did not work, and then along came the TV series *Singles* in which she won a whole new audience of admirers playing the glamorous divorcee, Pamela. One of her co-stars was Eamon Boland with whom she was reunited in *The Chief* when he was cast as Detective Chief Superintendent Jim Grey. *Singles* was followed by the critically acclaimed *Yesterday's Dreams* in which she was a woman torn between two men.

'*Yesterday's Dreams* brought me sackloads of letters from all over the world,' she says, 'and I still get people writing to me about it. That's great. I need such reassurance.'

Her confidence was boosted even more when she was offered the role of Elizabeth in *The Chief*.

'Tim is such an accomplished actor to work with,' she says, 'and I really enjoyed our scenes together. I know the part was a bit of a headache for the scriptwriters because what can you do with a Chief Constable's wife? She certainly couldn't sit at home and knit and say, "Had a good day at the office, dear?" Making her a GP was a good idea because it enabled her to be involved in local politics and events.'

Judy, as Dr Stafford, was also called on to intervene in arguments between her husband and their son, Tim (Ross Livingstone) who was accused of possessing cannabis. And then their daughter, Emma (Sara Griffiths) became involved in a student demonstration which had repercussions for the Chief, too.

'I sometimes used to think to myself, I wonder how any one woman could have coped with all that and be a good GP, too!' Judy says.

In the second series, John Stafford and his wife became noticeably closer, a factor that Judy was instrumental in introducing. She felt there had not been enough intimacy and humour in their relationship during the early episodes.

'When a couple have been together for as long a time as they have, they have a firm foundation and they share idiosyncracies and intimacies,' she says, explaining her reason for wanting a change of emphasis. 'We spoke to a Chief Constable who told us, "I do kiss my wife sometimes." So we decided to concentrate more on that aspect of their relationship. I think it presented the Chief as a more rounded character and it certainly gave their relationship depth. It made their home life more realistic, too.'

Judy had no hesitation in playing the intimate scenes this development demanded – in both the bathroom and the bedroom.

'Tim and I are seasoned performers and felt no embarrassment,' she smiles as if remembering those days on the set. 'In fact, I was so relaxed when they recorded a bedroom scene that the crew thought I had fallen asleep.

'I know you can tell if someone is pretending to be asleep because you can see them twitching. So I made a conscious effort

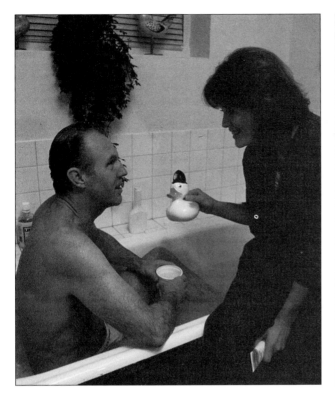

to relax so that I would look as if I was asleep. It was obviously convincing because the crew really thought I had dropped off! I must admit I thought it was not a bad way of making a living – being cosy under a warm duvet in a comfortable bed while it was cold outside.'

Off screen, Judy has continued to deal with whatever life has presented her. 'I have had an inner struggle in trying not to be the "good girl" all the time. I find it very hard to express my selfish needs, hard to express anger, hard to express my viewpoint if I think it's going to upset someone.'

Interestingly, for someone who has made quite a study of the role of the modern GP for her part in *The Chief*, she is now a committed enthusiast of alternative medicine. It was, in fact, this therapy which got her over her mystery bug which she feared might be M.E.

'It was a nightmare,' she says with a little shudder. 'I was desperately tired and run-down for weeks. I've always prided myself on being able to get over illnesses quickly in the past, but not this time. I was taking three different antibiotics but they made hardly any difference. I decided alternative therapy was the only answer.'

Judy explains that she was introduced to this form of medicine some years ago when she suffered from an agonizing pain in her

*Above Left: Judy Loe and Tim Pigott-Smith play an intimate scene in* The Chief.

*Above Right: The Staffords became closer in series two.*

spine which was cured by a form of Oriental massage known as Shiatsu. This involved her back being walked all over.

'When it seemed there was no cure for this illness and the date I had to start filming again was looming, I decided to give up the antibiotics. Instead I took a lot of rest, ate loads of fruit and vegetables and drank gallons of water to cleanse my system. It worked.

'It just goes to show we have to strengthen our natural resources rather than simply rely on drugs,' she enthuses.

By coincidence, as Judy and Tim Pigott-Smith were about to leave the series, she and Roy were also contemplating a new objective in their private life.

'Just as the Chief and Elizabeth were facing up to the fact that their children were leaving home and a new life in Brussels lay ahead, so Roy and I were contemplating the same situation with our two youngest, Kate and Will, both going off to University. It posed the question, "What are our ambitions?" We decided finding a new home abroad would be something exciting and set our target on Italy where we had found many secluded spots on holiday.

'So while Roy was busy on the *Inspector Morse* series, I went off to Italy and found this old farmhouse in the Umbrian mountains. It is in a breathtaking spot, overlooking the most incredible views – you can see Assissi from the windows. There is a lot of work to be done, but from the moment I saw the house I had this feeling it was meant to be the next stage in our lives. I felt we were on the road to something very important for us.'

Judy has, of course, no intentions of giving up acting and, like her co-star, would have liked the episodes in the third series to have followed the Staffords when they went to live and work in Brussels.

'There has been very little television which has explored characters working and living in the European community,' she says, 'and it would have been an interesting challenge. Especially for Elizabeth to have had to work out how she could continue her profession as a doctor when her husband was the Head of Europol. But Anglia had other ideas and so Eastland got a new Chief. One without a wife, too!'

## THE WOMAN WHO WOULD BE CHIEF

### Assistant Chief Constable Anne Stewart
### (Karen Archer)

The forceful, ambitious and attractive Assistant Chief Constable Anne Stewart came agonizingly close to becoming television's first female Chief Constable when the future of the series was being plotted two years ago. Although this ground-breaking idea did not come to be, the assertive, red-haired cop played by Karen Archer *did* become almost as popular with viewers as the Chief himself and made a major contribution to the success of the programme as a whole. The departure of Karen, a 'much underrated actress', to quote another press report, has undoubtedly been greeted with very mixed feelings by many viewers.

Karen's portrayal of the Assistant Chief Constable – who briefly became Acting Chief Constable during the transfer of power from Stafford to Alan Cade – was underpinned by her own strong conviction that a female could fill the post. The fact that there are two women in the police force already serving as deputies rather confirms this.

'I very strongly wanted Anne to be the first woman Chief Constable,' Karen says with the same look of determination in her blue eyes that she brought to the screen. 'Promotion from deputy was just one step away from that goal. I know there will be a female Chief Constable in real life eventually, and I wanted our programme to break new ground. We had pointed the way ahead in a number of the stories and this could have been the biggest breakthrough of all.'

In fact, producer Ruth Boswell did give serious thought to fulfilling Anne's dream.

'We discussed making Anne the Chief when we knew that Tim was going to leave,' she says. 'We gave the idea a lot of thought but rejected it in the end because we did not feel the audience would accept it. I know Karen would have liked to be the Chief, but I think it would have been too big a gamble.'

Both Ruth and Executive Producer Brenda Reid were, though, very sorry to lose Karen from the series which she had starred in from its inception.

Says Brenda, 'She was very popular with the audience, but to be fair we had reached the point where there was nowhere else for her character to go. We would have been forced to keep on repeating things, so with some regret we decided that Anne's life with the series had finished.

'Of course in the fourth series she was recruited into the Inspectorate which provided us with some nice added bits of drama. For here she was actually doing things like querying Cade's expenses, and from having worked under him she was now in the position to ask *why* he was doing something. Why he was behaving in a certain way. But, in the end, there was only so much that could be exploited out of that situation. I was sad when she left because there are so few policewomen at the top and I'm keen always to promote the idea that there *should* be.'

For Karen, working on *The Chief* was a joy because she lives not far from the Anglia studios in Upgate, Louth, in the beautiful Lincolnshire wolds. She is married to the actor David Collings, who starred in *Crime and Punishment* and the popular crime series, *Sapphire and Steel*. They have ten-year-old twins, Sam and Eliza. Much as Karen enjoyed her role, she admits candidly there is no way she would even consider a career in the police.

'Heaven forbid!' she laughs. 'I can't imagine anything worse. I am too lazy in real life ever to want the kind of responsibility Anne Stewart has. I am quite a strong, bossy and opinionated sort of person, but I can never imagine wanting to be absolutely in command, because there is no let up at all, it is a twenty-four-hours-a-day responsibility.

'I think it must be a very lonely job for a woman – no matter how much you play male camaraderie with the boys – and especially for someone as far up the career ladder as Anne, because there are no other women up there with you. So you are never really in either camp, and you are pretty isolated. The police would also be far too regimented for me.'

Despite her feelings, Karen researched her role with the same diligence as her co-star, Tim Pigott-Smith, talking at length to John Alderson and a number of senior women police officers.

'I have to admit that I found my views about the police changing as soon as I started mingling with senior officers,' she

*ACC Anne Stewart directing her forces in the Eastland headquarters' operations room.*

reflects. 'I spent two days with a woman superintendent at a West End station and joined a commander at the police training school in Hendon, Middlesex. They were both from very different backgrounds. One was highly academic, well-educated and taught philosophy. The other started as a WPC on the beat, but at thirty-five went off to the London School of Economics to take a law degree. She told me she had a very hard time in the Force, it had been a battle all the way.

'I sat in on meetings with her and I was very aware of how she responded to the men around the table as she put forward her views. She didn't raise her voice and there was quite a lot of humour and joking going on. I was quite impressed. I have to say I didn't see evidence myself of resentment, but I suppose there must be. I am a feminist with a small ''f'' and I think Anne is much the same. I now have a huge respect for what they do.'

Karen also has the added advantage of a policeman in the family.

'My younger brother, Justin, is a serving police sergeant in Oxfordshire,' she says, 'and he gave me some useful tips. He also told me that he and his colleagues watched the programme or videoed it if they were on duty. And none of them said, ''What a load of rubbish'', so I guess that means they all enjoyed it!'

The sum total of all this was that Karen ended up with a rather different outlook on the police.

'As a leftist-inclined *Guardian* reader, my views towards the police were rather questioning,' she says. 'But making *The Chief* has shown me that there are liberal, compassionate, caring and highly intelligent people in the Force.'

Karen's own career as an actress has embraced a wide range of roles, from the classical theatre to popular TV dramas. She actually began by training to be a drama teacher, but then found herself 'on the boards' in repertory at Oxford, Liverpool, Guildford and Kingston. This was followed by major roles in *Who's Afraid of Virginia Woolf*, *She Stoops to Conquer* and *Nicholas Nickleby*. A spell with the Royal Shakespeare Company took her to Stratford, New York and Los Angeles. Despite the fact that on television she has appeared in several police series – including *Rockliffe's Babies*, *Juliet Bravo* and *The Bill* (she was also 'Dirty Den's' solicitor in *East Enders*!) – it was not until *The Chief* that Karen actually put on a uniform for the first time.

The role of ACC Stewart proved a demanding and rewarding one in which she had to cope with the pressures of a top job, the prejudice and jealousy of senior male officers, and a wrecked marriage.

'The challenge for me was making Anne a figure of authority while still retaining her femininity,' she says. 'I believe it is possible to be strong without being butch. Yet you knew Anne had a battle to get where she was. Everyone leapt to their feet when she walked into a room. Everybody jumped, except the Chief. It's really amazing what a uniform can do for you. I felt full of authority as soon as I put it on. People told me they quaked in their shoes when I came near them!'

Karen believes that Anne had very strong ideals to get where she was. 'But she is also a wife and mum, which is where we probably took liberties with reality. Most successful women in the police tend not to have families. I don't believe she could have got that far if she did have children.

'Anne joined the Force because she wanted to do something different. She was aware that she was in an odd position, being in charge of all those men. There was a lot of feeling against her because she was a woman, and some of the officers used the deference they had to show as a cover for their resentment.'

The actress was delighted at the acceptance she received from viewers during the first series. Karen says that she had many letters urging her to 'take more direct control of matters instead of being the Chief's glorified PA'.

She even heard from the police themselves. 'Their comment was that at that rank I would have had a little bit more autonomy than

*A highly topical start to The Chief – Tim Pigott-Smith as John Stafford confronts rioting prisoners in the opening episode.*

*CC John Stafford and ACC Anne Stewart (Karen Archer) outside the Eastland HQ – aka Chelmsford Police Headquarters.*

*The Chief and his deputy inside the headquarters of Eastland – the Old Brewery set, in Norwich.*

**Opposite:** *Stafford and his family – Dr Elizabeth Stafford (Judy Loe), son, Tim (Ross Livingstone) and daughter, Emma (Sara Griffiths).*

Above: *Hunting a
murder suspect in
series two.*

Opposite: *Martin Shaw –
the dynamic second
chief constable of
Eastland makes his
debut in the third
series.*

Right: *A dramatic
day involving a
confrontation on an oil
rig introduced Alan
Cade to the Eastland
region. The new chief
constable with ACC
Anne Stewart.*

Opposite: *Alan Cade in the midst of the action, a habit that causes much controversy for the Eastland Chief.*

*Cade with one of the most important women in his life, Marie-Pierre Arnoux (Juliette Mole).*

*PRO Alison Dell (Ingrid Lacey) was also close to the Chief in series four.*

*Cade's new team at the top: DCC Wes Morton (Bosco Hogan) and DS Rose Penfold (Gillian Bevan), who join* The Chief *in series five.*

we showed in the first series. So the plots in the second were aimed to show Anne more in charge on her patch. I particularly relished the situations where she was able to come across as a woman who was competently in control in a positon of responsibility and not one having to defer to male superiority all the time.'

Anne Stewart's relationships with the two Chiefs whom she served could not have been more different. With Stafford there was a good understanding and though they fought quite a lot, she could always rely on his support. Alan Cade, on the other hand, had doubts about her from the first moment he took over the Eastland Force.

'Cade was very patronising,' says Karen looking back. 'When he agreed to give her a 100-day trial it was almost as if he was indulging a small child. So she went right out and proved herself, but he didn't stick to his side of the bargain.'

The strain of being loyal to the Force and her husband, Martin (David Cardy), a successful industrial chemist who put his career on hold in order to become a house father to their two children, of course lead eventually to the end of Anne's marriage. Karen remembers that period of the series very clearly, in particular because it generated newspaper stories in which she was described as the career-minded policewomen who had put promotion before her husband and children.

'The episodes about the marriage break-up were quite

*Above Left: The relationship between ACC Anne Stewart and her husband, Martin (David Cardy) was always uneasy and happy moments such as this were rare.*

*Above Right: Martin Stewart is forced to take care of the couple's children as the demands of his wife's job increase.*

upsetting,' she says, 'particularly where the children were involved. When you have children you are aware of how things can upset you. I found it easy to play those poignant scenes because I could see my own children in that situation. Children are very vulnerable and they know when something is wrong. But I don't think the boys who played my sons in the series realized quite how much they would be instrumental in pulling the heart strings.

'Some viewers may have thought Anne was cold and hard-hearted. But she had a strong sense of duty on a personal level and loyalty. So she was completely torn. Her husband was forcing her to choose between him and her job. She chose professional ethics, not realizing that this would be the last straw for her husband.'

In the third series, however, after being wary of any new relationship for some time, romance blossomed for Anne with the arrival of a new financial executive for the Eastland Force, David Kendal (Simon Slater).

'Her initial reaction was, "Who is this flash chap?" ' Karen smiles. 'But he made her laugh and was most disarming in an unexpected way. She didn't fall headlong in love, but as with all of us in life, love can strike at any time and one is always vulnerable to it. For an actor it is lovely to be able to soften the edges and underplay. Most of the time there was little opportunity for that because of the dramatic situations in which Anne Stewart found herself – barking out orders, tearing her hair out, climbing in and out of helicopters. So there was not much room for soft stuff.'

The development of this relationship in which David committed himself to Anne and her children – complete with 'a fair amount of snogging between us,' as Karen puts it – not only gave her the stability to accept the fresh challenge of the job in the Inspectorate (and ultimately her departure from the series), but had an amusing side affect on her real life in Louth. For between jobs she often works as a supply teacher at a local primary school.

'I'm the kind of person who hates to sit around doing nothing,' she explains, 'so if I haven't got any acting work I may as well be teaching. Some of the children recognized me from *The Chief*. They would come up to me in the playground and ask if I was on television – but when I said I was they were puzzled because I was known as Mrs Collings at school! The series was on a bit late for my twins to watch – and it was very distracting watching with them, anyway. They were constantly asking how I did a scene, who the man was kissing me and did I know him!'

One of Karen's most vivid memories from her time working on *The Chief* occurred during the filming of an episode about the seizure of a North Sea oil rig by some disgruntled employees. She was then on her '100-day trial period' and determined to succeed.

'In the story I had to fly out to the rig to try and break the deadlock,' she says, her eyes sparkling at the memory. 'There was a Force 9 gale blowing as I was winched down on to the rig from a helicopter. They told me to drop down flat on the deck when I landed and grip the ropes or I would be blown off.

'I loved it and I didn't feel frightened at all! The only problem was I had to wear this big rubber suit which hurt my feet as I had to run along the corrugated iron staircase!'

While Karen can still smile at this memory, another she found deeply upsetting. This was the dilemma Anne Stewart faced when ordering the killing of a sniper who has been marauding around the Eastland countryside taking pot shots at all and sundry – something, she says, that is completely at odds with her strongly pacifist beliefs.

'I found the scene very upsetting to do because I could never, ever cold-bloodedly kill someone,' she says, her eyes hardening. 'If there was a war I would be a conscientious objector. You see, I feel very strongly that the further we go towards the American style of policing, the worse it is going to be for us all. I am deeply anti-violence. I do understand if there are people on the streets with guns you have to have an armed police force to deal with them. But I believe you have to take the line of least resistance. I am fiendishly opposed to relaxing gun laws – they should be tightened up now. The more guns there are, who ever has got them, the more dangerous it is for all of us. The fewer guns, in uniform or out of uniform, the better.

'In the original script there was actually no allusion to the enormity of what Anne Stewart had done in ordering the sniper to be killed,' Karen continues, 'and she just went on to talk about her job prospects. So I asked for a piece to be written into the scene. I felt it was important that we saw Anne Stewart, if not suffering remorse, then at least being anxious about whether she had done the right thing. Also displaying some of the human vulnerability a person would feel about taking someone's life. That was how we actually came to have that moment of questioning in the story.'

Off-screen Karen is also deeply moved by tragedy of any kind, and raised several thousand pounds for sick children in Romania. A large slice of this came from other members of the cast and crew of *The Chief* whom she urged to support the cause by putting money into a small plastic bucket she always kept close to the set whenever they were filming. Later she made several journeys with other charity workers from Lincolnshire:

*Above: Anne Stewart, flying to a dangerous mission on a high-jacked North Sea oil rig.*

*Right: After the break-up of her marriage, DCC Anne Stewart found new romance with David Kendal (Simon Slater), the new financial executive to the Eastland force.*

driving over 3,000 miles with supplies for a primitive, ill-equipped hospital. It was an experience she admits made her cry. Karen has also campaigned against the shutting down of Queen Charlotte's Maternity Hospital in Hammersmith where her own children were born.

Although she makes no bones about her disappointment at being written out of the series which she helped to establish, Karen is pleased that her role has helped to enhance the public image of women in the police force. Indeed her performance has built on the achievements of Jill Gascoigne and Anna Carteret who launched a new TV era for women as police officers in the Eighties in *The Gentle Touch* and *Juliet Bravo*.

Interestingly, according to a Home Office statement, series such as these have encouraged far more female recruits to the police force – a recent survey showing that women now comprise 12.1

percent of the Metropolitan Police compared to only 6.7 percent in 1978.

'I was disappointed by the decision that Anne had to go because it meant we could have seen a woman rising through the ranks to the top job in a police series for the very first time on television,' she reflects. 'But it was nice to have breached this confined, circumscribed, bureaucratic set-up, where you have to play by the rules which are male dominated and male dictated, and show what a really determined woman could do. There are still only two women Assistant Chief Constables in the country, out of 36, and no woman has gone any higher. But I'm sure it's only a matter of time before the police – and television – has a female Chief.'

And her own plans for the future? She hopes for more work in the classical theatre and on television.

'I would also like to do something interesting about a woman *not* in uniform,' she says giving a smile that is both assertive and charming. 'I would love to do something which gives you humour and romance.'

# A STRAIGHT-DOWN-THE-LINE COPPER
## DCS Jim Gray (Eamon Boland)

Detective Chief Superintendent Jim Gray was at the centre of one of the most controversial subjects tackled by *The Chief* during its early days – the police force and the Freemasons. He was the officer faced with a crisis of conscience when his loyalties to the force came into conflict with those he felt he owed to a member of the lodge to which he also belonged.

Arguments about the police and the involvement of officers in masonry has been a long-running issue in the media as well as one of the underlying elements in *The Chief* – perhaps most forceably since Alan Cade took office, for he, more than his predecessor, is personally offended by secret organizations and will not tolerate any unfair advantages operating within his force.

Jim Gray, in fact, moved to centre stage in the unfolding drama of *The Chief* as early as episode five of the first series when John Stafford was in the midst of fighting off a dirty-tricks campaign by another of his officers, Chief Inspector George Hedger (Trevor Byfield). At the same time, DCS Gray suddenly discovered that a fellow mason, businessman Howard Reeves (Ken Farrington), was being investigated for fraud and felt compelled to warn him.

This clash of loyalties offered a fascinating challenge for the versatile Eamon Boland in the playing of his character – and one which he was able to sustain very successfully until the parting of the ways when Cade arrived in Eastland.

'Jim was a very straight-down-the-line policeman,' says Eamon. 'In many ways he was quite an old-fashioned copper. There were times when he felt he was being put in situations which he didn't relish because the Chief was a very radical person. He really didn't see eye to eye with Stafford on certain things and that gave an edge to their relationship.'

Eamon, who was born in Manchester in 1947 of Irish descent, is something of a complex character himself, having actually begun his career as a history teacher. Indeed, he admits, he might easily not have become an actor at all.

'I didn't learn drama at school,' he says, 'although I liked reading plays. I never thought of myself as an actor – all I used to do was clown around and make the other children laugh. Then at teachers' training college I took drama as a substitute subject and was hooked on it. I thought, "What do I do now?"'

'You see I enjoyed teaching. I felt committed to it, I had good qualifications and I was a good teacher. I taught for nearly two years and then applied for a place at drama school. I couldn't get another grant but they offered me a scholarship so I spent about a year and a half driving lorries for the money.'

Eamon was twenty-five when he entered the Bristol Old Vic. This was followed by several years in rep, after which he joined Joan Littlewood's Theatre Workshop in Stratford, East London, and made his debut in 1976 in *Funny Peculiar*. The experience he gained in this famous little company earned him a role in the award-winning version of Samuel Beckett's *Coming Clean* and then the drama, *Masterpieces* at the Royal Court.

It was in 1980 that he gained his first experience of crime drama on television in the Thames series *Fox*, directed by Jim Goddard and starring Peter Vaughan. He played one of seven tough East London brothers. Violence was also a keynote in the controversial BBC thriller *Crossfire*, shown in 1988, in which he played a backroom civil servant, Freddie Ross, caught up in the ongoing conflict in Ireland, and whose job is tracking down fugitive IRA terrorists.

'*Crossfire* attracted its fair share of controversy at the time,' Eamon recalls, drawing a parellel with *The Chief*. 'It first arose about a year earlier when we were filming in Northern Ireland. Apparently complaints were made about the serial's allegedly over-sympathetic portrayal of the IRA. Some changes were made – "to obtain maximum authenticity" is how they put it officially – but the end result was that *Crossfire* was not shown until April 1988.

'Obviously when you get a good part like that you want to be seen,' he says, 'but as an actor I don't think I'd have become involved with it if it had been one-sided one way or the other.'

Eamon certainly had no idea that controversy would follow him to *The Chief* – but once again he faced it with the equanimity that has been his trademark on and off the screen.

'I'm always quite content to wait for the right part to come along,' he says. 'If I'm not working I'm always glad of the opportunity to go climbing or fell walking.'

He certainly found Detective Sergeant Gray a good part, however – and working on the series had a special attraction for him because he actually lives in a centuries old timbered cottage in one of the most beautiful communities in Eastland: the former Suffolk wool town of Lavenham, still full of Tudor buildings reminiscent of the Middle Ages. So playing the part only involved a pleasant drive across the picturesque countryside to Anglia's studios in Norwich or whatever location in the region was being used. Quite a change from the long distances he had had to travel on many earlier engagements.

Talking of the Detective Chief Superintendent, Eamon says, 'Jim Gray was not afraid to roll up his sleeves and get on with the job. He was a hard-working copper dedicated to the police, and the masonic incident was his one fall from grace.'

Controversy also marked Eamon's departure from the series when Martin Shaw took over the central role. A report in the *Glasgow Evening Times* of 10 April 1993 maintained that he was being ousted as a result of a wage cut. Under a headline, 'UNFAIR: MARTIN TAKES OVER FROM TIM – AND EAMONN'S [SIC] WAGES ARE SLASHED', the paper stated:

'It's not just on screen that the departure of one chief and the arrival of another has caused ructions. Eamonn Boland who plays Det. Chief Supt Jim Gray, claims he's been forced to take a drop in wages from the previous two series of *The Chief* because Anglia has to pay so much to secure the services of Martin Shaw. Anglia deny the claim and say that everyone in the series was, "paid the rate for the job".'

In fact, Eamon wanted to leave and Jim Gray's departure was used by the scriptwriters to reflect the growing influence of privatization on the police force. The Detective Chief Superintendent was offered more money to join a security firm as a director and, fed up with the politics and jockeying for position, decided to quit for the private sector.

Eamon has subsequently worked in several other police series – including *The Bill* where he recently turned up in an episode called 'Legacy' playing the role of a police 'grass' or informer at the mercy of a tough DS – and remains as phlegmatic as ever about his own future. 'As I said, I'm quite happy waiting for the right parts to come along. If the worse comes to the worst, I still have my heavy goods vehicle licence!'

# 6

# CADE'S COUNTRY
## A Night Shoot with the Chief

The July evening was warm and the skies clear, a pale moon illuminating the undulating Norfolk countryside with its great tracts of farmland dotted by occasional small communities such as Hingham. Deep in the heart of Eastland, this sleepy rural village lies 15 miles from Norwich and is like many others in the Chief's country: a cluster of elegant period houses at the heart, and behind them some little streets of modern, semi-detached properties. Adjoining the village is a small industrial estate (engineering, shoe manufacture and a horse box centre) and beyond this, hundreds of acres of wheat now in the process of being harvested.

In Hingham itself on this balmy mid-summer evening, there are the usual convivial groups of customers to be found in the bar of the fine old coaching inn, The White Hart, or else the more modern pub, the Eight Ringers. Some residents are even taking advantage of the good weather to stroll around the market place past the rows of elegant Georgian houses which give the locality its unspoiled look of having changed very little since the eighteenth century. At one side of the carefully maintained green stands Lincoln's Tea & Coffee Shop with its sign of entwined Union Jack and American flags which serve as an ever-present reminder of the town's links with the pioneer days of America.

For it was a descendent of Samuel Lincoln of Hingham, an early emigrant to the New World, who became one of America's most famous presidents, Abraham Lincoln. The town itself also gave its name to Hingham in Massachusetts, a fact commemorated by a granite bolder presented by the present citizens of Hingham, USA to their namesakes in exchange for an old mounting block that once stood outside the blacksmith's forge.

In actual fact, there could be few small communities more typical of those to be found throughout Eastland than this one which has managed to combine the elegance of the past with the necessities of the present. Yet on this otherwise unremarkable

*East Anglian Daily Times, Monday, July 18, 1994  Page 9*

# Armed police in raid on 'gunmen' hous[

## BY AMANDA CRACK

ARMED police sur-rounded a house on a busy town estate in a search for two suspected gunmen.

Police said the raid in Steward Close, on the Nowton Estate, Bury St Edmunds, came after a man was allegedly threatened with a hand-gun in the early hours of Saturday.

As police mounted the operation, neighbours lined the paths, concerned for their safety.

One mother said her children had been playing outside when the armed response units arrived and had not been allowed back to their house while police sealed the road off.

"The first thing I knew that there was something going on was when I heard a police loud-speaker saying: 'Will you come out?'" she said.

"There was an armed response unit, the lot. They broke the door down but there was no-one there."

Police are believed to have arrived at about 10am and to have left the scene nearly three hours later.

The raid came after the alleged threat in Fornham Road, Bury, at 2.20am. The man was not hurt but was said to have been very frightened by his ordeal.

A police s[...] "Following on f[...] a police operat[...] to arrest two ot[...] suspected of b[...] who were b[...] premises in Ja[...]

"A search v[...] to locate the[...] were used i[...] ensure the sa[...] cerned."

They late[...] tion hand[...] offensive w[...]

Two Bur[...] year-old, w[...] bail yeste[...] investigati[...] carried ou[...]

night in July 1994 its peace and tranquility are about to be shattered by an act of violence which will have far-reaching implications for the Chief and his force.

For it is in Hingham that the production team have chosen to film the explosive opening scenes of the fifth series – to be specific at a late-Georgian manor house, Hardingham Hall, just over a mile from the town and set deep in its own fields and meadows.

There is something almost apposite about the drama which is to unfold here. For a former seventeenth century rector, Robert Peck, was noted as a man of outspoken mind who rebelled against his superiors and finally emigrated to America to find freedom of expression. Tonight, the equally controversial Chief Constable of Eastland is to be drawn into a confrontation of his own: in this instance with a trio of armed criminals disturbed in the middle of a robbery.

It is also a night on which the prescience of yet another story about the Chief which had been written months earlier is to be underlined by actual events. For as I drove out to the location and stopped to buy a newspaper in Hingham, the front page headlines of the local *Evening News* proclaimed, 'CITY GUN DRAMA', and reported how, earlier in the day, armed police officers had responded to a call to the Grapes Hill area of Norwich where a man had been spotted with a gun . . .

*As the shots rang out on the set of* The Chief, *the same was happening in real life, as a gunman was spotted in the local area.*

Hardingham Hall is not an unfamiliar sight to observant television viewers. Parts of it have already been seen in Anglia productions such as *Tales of the Unexpected* and the series based on Jilly Cooper's best-selling novel, *Riders.* Approached by a sweeping gravel driveway through a screen of tall pine trees, it immediately impresses the visitor as a building with all the hallmarks of style and taste. The ivy-covered walls, a vaulted, porticoed front and a coat of arms above the doorway all combine to make it highly photogenic. Out of sight at the rear are an impressive open-air swimming pool, a cluster of outbuildings and a spacious paddock.

Tonight there are also a number of other less expected things hidden from view at the back of the Hall – namely all the paraphernalia that is essential to the making of a major television drama series on location. The unit office caravans, mobile changing quarters for the actors, generator lorries and a number of vehicles belonging to the production team which are crammed with sound, lighting and camera equipment. Plus a double-decker canteen bus which will keep up a supply of hot food and drinks for the unit of seventy-five people all through the night ahead.

For the episode in question the Hall has been renamed Brackley Grange and is now the home of a wealthy entrepreneur, Charles Wadlow, who is away on a business tirp to China, having left his wife behind on her own. Shortly the house will be broken into by three armed villains, Bernie Chandler (their leader, played by Ken Hutchison), Jakie Hunt (Richard Haddon) and 'Dick' Barton (a tongue-in-cheek acknowledgement to the famous stiff-upper-lip radio detective of the forties, played by Cameron-Ian Lock) who force their way in and take Mrs Wadlow (Michelle Montague) prisoner. Their actions will form the core of the unfolding drama – along with the unexpected arrival of the Chief and his young driver which will end in tragedy . . .

The initial scene to be filmed actually takes place inside the house in one of the front rooms where the young men break in. Here director Tom Cotter puts the four actors through the gruelling ill-treatment of Mrs Wadlow as they force her to reveal the combination to her husband's safe. The oppressive sense of terror is realistically generated by the actors themselves, while the illusion that night has already fallen has been artifically created by blacking-out all the Hall's downstairs windows. The final ingredient is Tom Cotter's own skill at motivation.

Tom, an energetic, methodical Scot, has had a long career as a director which has taken him as far afield as Hollywood – where he worked on the prestigious TV mystery programme, *The Ray Bradbury Theatre* – and close to home in Norwich where he was one of the team who made Anglia's long-running and very successful thriller series, *Tales of the Unexpected*. He is a man with a special expertise at making fast-paced drama and creating a sense of mounting terror on film.

'Working at night has its advantages and disadvantages,' Tom explains as those around him set up the scene of the robbery for a second take. 'When it's dark you can use this to really heighten the viewer's feeling of danger. But if you've got a tight shooting schedule then certain scenes have to be done while it's still light and that's when the lighting guys earn their crust. With this first story we are aiming to grab the attention of our audience the moment they switch on.'

The four actors re-enact the break-in once again. The air in the room is heavy and close, and in the darkened hallway the crew huddled behind the camera are sweating almost as much as the three young men under their balaclava helmets. Michelle Montague is once more manhandled, bound and gagged – this time to Tom Cotter's evident satisfaction.

'Cut,' he says. 'OK. Let's move outside.' The sighs of relief all round are universal.

All of the rest of the night's filming will take place on the driveway in front of the main entrance. Circular in shape, it is surrounded by a neat lawn, several beds of roses and an ornamental pond complete with fountain. As the shadows of evening begin to creep in at 9pm the setting takes on a whole new atmosphere – one which is heightened by the strategic positioning of some huge floodlights amidst the trees.

It is at this moment, too, that Martin Shaw arrives on the location and the excitement that had enlivened the sets in 'The Old Brewery' is evident again. As usual he makes time for a few jokes with the crew members before getting an update on the progress of shooting from Tom Cotter. Then he goes off to change in his personal caravan, designated 'MH' (Motor Home). Once again the change from casual clothes into the immaculate, dark-suited figure of Alan Cade seems to be both physical and mental. In the encroaching darkness, his stocky figure becomes the focus of everyone's attention while the next scene is rehearsed and the camera and lights are given their final adjustments.

According to the storyline, Cade has chanced upon the events unfolding in Brackley Grange while on his way home from some firearms training. The Chief has, it seems, been urged to carry a gun for personal protection after receiving a death threat from a crank. Despite this, he remains unconvinced about the value of the police being armed, even in the face of an increase in violent crimes in Eastland.

His worst nightmare is, however, now about to unfold as his chauffeur-driven Jaguar, G142 FVW, with his driver, Jack Sayers

*The arming of the police is a subject of continuing concern for Alan Cade, here in a police bullet-proof vest.*

(Dean Lepley) at the wheel, approaches Hingham. For over the radio, Cade hears that a patrolling Panda car has noticed that Brackley Grange is in darkness whereas it is normally floodlit. Although the two police officers in the Panda, a constable (Ian Driver) and a woman PC (Isabel Murphy), have not been able to get any reply in response to ringing the doorbell, the Chief decides to investigate for himself. Pulling up in front of the house, he reassures the two somewhat surprised young officers: 'Let's take another look – so he'll feel he's getting good value for his Council tax.'

With the aid of a flashlight, the young policeman then goes around the far side of the house and, through a gap in the curtains, spots the three men stuffing money from the safe into bags. He sprints back to Cade, shouting out that there are armed robbers inside.

A moment later, sensing they have been spotted, the three men run out of the house and appear on the driveway. In the next few seconds, the tranquillity of a summer evening in Hingham is shattered.

Aware that the robbers have seen his young officers, Cade at once dives on to the grass and assumes the firing position. He yells out at the masked figures: 'Armed police! Don't move.'

For a split second there is a stillness around the set that can almost be felt. The leader, Chandler, raises his gun which glints in the half-light. It is an Uzi, the ugly, snub-nosed Isreali carbine so favoured by criminals and terrorists because of its rapid, scattering firepowers. A vicious burst of fire reverberates noisily around the set. It narrowly misses Cade but strikes the Panda car where the young WPC is crouched.

So realistic is the effect of this gun going off that some pheasants nesting in the copse behind the driveway can be heard rising with screams of alarm. And one can only imagine the look of puzzlement that must have crossed the faces of anyone who happened to be within earshot of the blast as it echoed beyond the walls of Hardingham Hall.

Cade has now leapt to his feet again and is running, half-crouched, towards his car which is on the move. Jack Sayers has realized the danger his boss is in and is speeding towards him with the passenger door thrown open. As the Chief dives on to the front seat another burst of fire catches the Jaguar and strikes the driver. Without so much as a sound, Sayers falls sideways against the doorjam.

The scene reaches its dramatic climax as Cade wrestles the vehicle to a standstill. As he does so he sees that his young companion has been hit and is badly, perhaps fatally, injured. He takes Jack's unconscious, bloodied head tenderly in his hands and

lets out a cry of anguish. Behind him, the villain's silver-grey
BMW can be seen speeding off down the driveway with its haul of
a quarter of a million pounds . . .

The filming of those dramatic scenes which will occupy less than
ten minutes on the screen were the result of almost nine hours of
highly artistic and technical skills. A mixture of Maggie Allen's
evocative script, some powerfully-orchestrated acting, the talents
of a stunt team, and the artistry of the lighting, sound and camera
crews. Also brought into play was one of the modern marvels of
filming, a tiny 'lipstick' camera (so called because of its
resemblance to that familiar female acccessory) which was
installed on the dashboard of the Jaguar to catch the Chief's
agony in close-up.

The two stunt doubles who impersonated Cade and Jack Sayers
(Steve Whyment and Neil Finnighan) had been rehearsing the skid
around the driveway and the Chief's desperate jump into the
passenger seat since the late afternoon. (No such risks could be
run by Martin Shaw or even the ill-fated Dean Lepley.) A similar
deception was also worked by Stunt co-ordinator Alan Stuart with
the gunfire. Blanks were obviously fired by Chandler's gun, but
the ingenuity of modern technology enables these to be seen on film
as bullets exploding, in a shower of sparks and broken glass, on
hitting the windows of the Jaguar and the Panda.

*The stunt team set up
a dramatic shoot-out
between the police and
villains for an episode
of* The Chief.

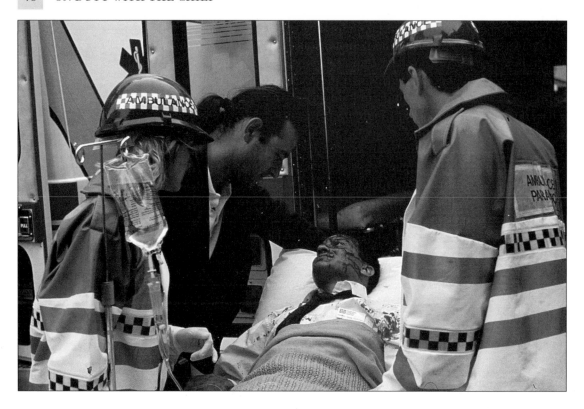

*A shooting incident in the fourth series leaves at least one seriously injured.*

Some of the gunshots were produced by small charges fitted around the front of the cars and then detonated electronically on cue. The remainder were actually tiny missiles fired from a gun of the type used in the 'paint ball' weapon games. These plastic-coated projectiles consist of a mixture of explosives which throw out a shower of sparks the instant they come into contact with any surface. On impacting, however, their composition is such as to offer no danger of injury to human flesh – or even the risk of leaving a mark on the vehicles' expensive paintwork!

Such stunts are not without their risks, of course, and on call the whole night was a professional armourer, John Warner, who supervised the firing of the Uzi and advised Alan Stuart on the trajectories of the imaginary bullets. Two members of the St John's Ambulance Brigade were among the onlookers just in case – but like the rest of us were only called upon to watch with admiration as the shooting was successfully completed.

The scene, for all its elements of deception, was played with consummate skill by Martin Shaw who in doing so revealed not only his agility but also how fit he keeps himself. At the final cut he looked as exhilarated as everyone else at how smoothly the complex not to mention expensive stunt had worked. And as everyone trooped off around the back of the Hall for coffee and a hot snack break, his sense of humour got the better of him once again and he could not resist calling out to the three 'villains' who had now returned in the BMW and were busy removing their hoods.

'La-la-lal-la-la,' he hummed the familiar jibe, 'you missed me!'

Throughout the filming of *The Chief* which takes up to six months of each year, Martin actually lives in Norfolk in a cottage at Watton which is convenient for both location shoots like the one at Hingham and the Norwich studios which are under 20 miles away. Apart from the convenience of the place, it has also enabled him to get a feeling of life in 'Eastland' as well as satisfying his passion for flying at the nearby aero club in Swanton Morley. (See 'Airborn With The Chief'.)

Martin can appear at times a brooding, almost intimidating figure. That is until he smiles. He is certainly a man of hidden emotional depths and one of this great skills as an actor is the ability to make even the smallest gesture give the clue to an entire scene. Indeed, as I had just witnessed, he can switch from the terror of being confronted by a gun-wielding villain to the heart-stopping despair of a man watching a colleague die – and feeling responsible for it – with a practised ease that only a lifetime of working at his art can have made possible.

It was, indeed, this ability to bring his own kind of dynamism to a part that made him accept the challenge of taking on the role of *The Chief* in the shadow of another well-known actor.

'Tim is someone I admire and I enjoyed the first two series of *The Chief* because of him,' he says in his softly measured voice. 'What struck me was that it wasn't just another police show. It examined a lot of the current issues and controversies surrounding today's police.

'But my character is very different from Tim's – and he and I are very different actors, anyway. Stafford was a methodical policeman and Cade thought of him as a bit of a plodder because he likes to take calculated risks. Cade is actually very dynamic and charismatic; a bit of a flash Harry, in fact, but absolutely dedicated to liberty, equality and justice.

'I suppose coming from the Met, he was a bit frustrated that he couldn't just leap into a car, turn on the blue light and siren, and career down the high street and start laying into the villains. He missed being directly at the sharp end.'

Interesting words from a man who had just survived a hail of bullets – but intriguing as a pointer to the fact that in the new series the Chief will find himself closer to the heart of the action.

Like his predecessor, Martin also did a lot of preliminary research into the life of a Chief Constable with the help of John Alderson and by meeting a number of acting policemen. He was anxious, he says, to see how far he could 'push the limits of the character' and the result is an amalgam of all the people he spoke to. Though perhaps one man more than any other.

'I met Peter Ryan, the Chief Constable of Norfolk, several times and observed him at work,' Martin recalls. 'He became my main model for Cade. He is glamorous, has a similar kind of cropped hairstyle, and dresses well.

'One of the things that did worry me when I took the role was I could see from the way it was written, with Cade as a glamour boy, that people would say it was not real, that policemen are not like this, that we were portraying Cade in this way only to sell the programme. But in fact some of the policemen I met were actually more interesting and glamorous than Alan Cade, right down to the power dressing!'

He smiles at the memory of those early encounters with serving officers in both London and East Anglia. 'I visited New Scotland Yard and I was amazed. I wanted to see what today's senior officers were really like and I soon discovered that there is no sign of good old PC Plod! The top coppers I talked to were intelligent and sophisticated.

'I admit I was really surprised at some of the languorous intellects I encountered. I had this preconceived notion that some of the high-ups were going to be rather dull and desk-bound, but not a bit of it. There was one senior officer in the Metropolitan Police who had an office like an antiques mall, wore a designer suit and a hand painted silk tie, and used classical references in his conversation like a university professor. He was actually the man who set up the national criminal intelligence service. Another senior policeman who was the British representative at the trial of Noriega is a visiting fellow at three universities.

'All my ideas were completely shattered by those men. I remember thinking to myself, ''Where *have* these guys been hiding themselves?'' On TV all you see is a particular type. I think it raises a lot of questions about the police's PR. Surely these are the people who the public should be seeing if they want to improve their image? There is no doubt in my mind that today's top coppers are genuine high flyers.'

Martin says that he set out to try and make his Chief match these role-models – although privately he admits he would probably be intimidated if he met Cade in real life. And policing is certainly a job he could *never* do.

'The form is too rigid,' he explains. 'I would find it too upsetting. And it's not creative enough for me. But playing Cade is satisfying because I like to access those parts of myself which affect people. That's what my job is about, affecting people. There's a part of my nature that hates to play safe, that likes to take risks.'

Turning to the development of his character, Martin continues, 'Right from the start Cade has been battling to fill a pressure job. On the one hand he wants to be in at the sharp end and refuses to hide behind a desk. But on the other, he has to cope with relentless political manoeuvreing. The Home Office had hoped they had appointed someone they could manipulate easily, but he soon proved to be more unconventional and dangerous than Stafford ever was.

'That's another reason I wanted the part. Being a senior policeman these days is demanding, difficult and deeply interesting. That and the fact *The Chief* is radical, and I think it is time that somebody did something a bit radical in serious television. To try and put across a radical point of view on a weekly basis is good and healthy.'

By a curious twist of fate, no sooner had Martin begun to get to grips with his role than Peter Ryan announced he was leaving his post. The *Eastern Daily Press* was quick to pick up the juxtaposition in its story of 31 March 1993, under the headline, 'TV COP SHOW A MIRROR IMAGE'.

'As Norfolk police await a new supremo, Anglia TV has revealed that *The Chief* drama series will resume next month with the East Anglian force losing its high-profile head. The TV trailer, a day after the news that Norfolk Chief Constable Peter Ryan is to quit for a £50,000-a-year post in charge of police training, suggests that fact can mirror fiction. Or vice versa.'

Martin had, however, already completed his preparation and was more than ready to launch Cade on to the screen. He liked the idea that the new Chief would receive a frosty reception in Eastland from a force wary of his charismatic style and glamorous designer image.

'They saw him at first as one of the Brylcream and glamour boys of the Metropolitan Police,' Martin recalls of his introduction, 'and they had their doubts about whether he could do the job. Eastland is pretty staid and they resented a new boy arriving and telling them what to do. So right away he had that problem to contend with.

'I particularly enjoyed that aspect because he soon ruffled a lot of feathers. In fact Cade had to spell out his philosophy, letting his men know all about his high moral code and the fact he didn't like wearing uniforms and didn't want to be saluted!'

A typical piece of dialogue from Martin's debut story exemplified everything he stood for: 'I'm not a lumberjack, forester, reindeer or bearer of the Fifteenth Candle. I don't subscribe to coppers belonging to secret organizations. Any form of corruption will have to face the courts and me, without mercy. Promotion does not lie in that vale, either.'

*Cade arriving to take up his position as the new Chief Contable of Eastland, in 1992.*

Martin has shown a similar dedication and individuality in his approach to his own profession as an actor. And like Tim Pigott-Smith he showed the same determination to shake off an image which may have made him well-known but has haunted him ever since: that of the CI5 man Ray Doyle in *The Professionals*. It was a role, he says, in which he felt he was 'appropriated like a doll' and one he prefers to forget. His other work on the stage and on TV can indeed be seen on closer examination to have been remarkably varied and often very adventurous . . .

Martin was born in Birmingham in 1945 just as the Second World War was coming to an end. At school he enjoyed English language, writing and poetry, but it was drama that really fascinated him. He appeared in several school plays where, he recalls, 'for the first time in my life I discovered something I could do really well'. Instead of encouraging this, however, Martin's careers teacher dismissed the idea of becoming an actor as 'silly and far too precarious', and recommended he became a librarian. At this, the young boy evidenced for the first time the relentless desire to be his own man which has guided his adult life. He took a job briefly as a sales clerk and then at 18 won a place at the London Academy of Music and Dramatic Art.

Martin's first job in the theatre was as an assistant stage manager at Hornchurch Repertory, which he followed with a number of parts in the company's productions. Next he went to the Bristol Old Vic and from that forcing house of talent was able to take on a whole range of parts including several of the classics at the National Theatre and the Royal Court; following these with contemporary dramas such as *Other People's Money* in which he played a Wall Street asset-stripper; Dennis Potter's *Cream in My Coffee*; and his unforgettable performance as Elvis Presley in *Are You Lonesome Tonight?* He still recalls today how it would take him ninety minutes before every performance to transform himself into the bloated and drug-dependent singer who was at the end of his life. But he was rewarded with rave reviews and packed houses.

In the summer of 1994, before returning to make the fifth series of *The Chief*, he also received excellent notices for his season in *Rough Justice*, Terence Frisby's thought-provoking drama about a man accused of child murder who decides to represent himself without realizing the onslaught he will face from the prosecuting counsel.

Martin's other television work has included appearances in *Z-Cars*, *Sutherland's Law*, *The Duchess of Duke Street* and starring roles in *The Hound of the Baskervilles* (as Sir Henry Baskerville), Captain Scott of the Antarctic in *The Last Place on Earth* and a Tory MP in *For The Greater Good*.

Politics, in fact, is a subject that has long interested him and he believes that Cade would actually make an excellent politician.

'I'm fascinated by politics,' he admits. 'When they started broadcasting the proceedings of the House of Commons I had the television switched on half an hour before the transmission. I was pacing up and down, twitching and itching for it to start, as you would for the Cup Final.

'But I couldn't be a politician,' insists the man who now spends a part of every episode of *The Chief* battling with whose who reside in the corridors of power at Westminster. 'I haven't the capacity for dissimulation they have. I can only operate from the truth, and they won't. There may be some I am doing a great disservice to. Ken Livingstone tells the truth unashamedly and without fear; therefore he will never get anywhere, he is too dangerous.

'I've also come to realize more and more that the job of a senior police officer, particularly a Chief Constable, is a political one. The political motives put forward by the writers and producers of *The Chief* are largely those which I embrace myself, so it gives me an opportunity to articulate my own thoughts. I actually think Cade would be better suited to something bigger in politics; he would make a wonderful cabinet minister. I can just envisage him going into politics.'

*It did not take Alan Cade long to demonstrate that he would be a radical and controversial new Chief of Eastland.*

*An off-duty moment for the glamorous Alan Cade with his long-time partner, Marie-Pierre Arnoux (Juliette Mole) – a relationship that was soon to be torn apart by the stresses of his job.*

Martin has, of course, gradually developed new elements of Cade's personality throughout the series. The tough-talking image on his arrival in the third series, for example, was somewhat softened in the fourth.

'I thought it was very important to show the human dimension of Cade's character, because you had Mr Steel Eyes in the office and you needed to see Mr Softy at home,' he says. 'I think it is important for viewers to know that top jobs are done by people with human frailties, too.'

Another side of Cade was seen in the albeit brief relationships that followed the break-up with his long-time partner, Marie-Pierre Arnoux (Juliette Mole). Firstly, with the PRO Alison Dell (Ingrid Lacey), and then his sparky encounters with the barrister, Gemma Marshall (Maureen Beattie), which promised so much at the end of the fourth series but are not going to materialize in the fifth. His paternal side has also been explored in the similarly brief reappearance of his daughter, Elena (Louisa Haigh), a reminder of his carefree and radical youth before the law became his whole world.

'Of course, Cade will continue to be as controversial and radical as ever,' Martin says, 'there is no way he could be anything else. And even when he comes under fire, he is never going to be restrained and is no more likely to toe the line. Nor is the friction with the Home Office likely to change. They are still trying to put forward the views of the Tory party and Cade has his own way and views. So there is conflict between the independence of the Chief Constable and the lack of independence that would be desired by government forces.'

It is quite evident from these remarks that Martin has a very clear vision of his character – although he is not quite sure just how much is him and how much has been created.

'Cade's strength is that he is not ambitious in the traditional sense of the word. He has a very strong sense of self, who he is and what his needs are. He would be pleased to go further up the ladder, but he doesn't need it. I think he is terribly idealistic. That is probably a very difficult thing to be if you are a Chief Constable. In the end, it is very hard for me to know whether I have invented it all or whether it is really me. I suspect it is a combination of both.

'I certainly share his frustration and irritation with bureaucracy, and his pragmatism. It's rather fun playing at somebody who does this – as long as I have the safety of not having to face the consequences!'

One consequence of Martin's actions on the screen has, however, been that he is now recognized in the street as *The Chief* and has found himself on the receiving end of the odd practical joke or two. He is, though, more than a match for anyone who chooses to take him on.

'We were filming in this small Norfolk village last year,' he recalls. 'I was in full uniform. Just as we finished, these two local bobbies drove up and made some crack. I turned sharply round and told them they were on a double yellow line. You should have seen their faces!'

Like Tim Pigott-Smith, Martin has also had his run-ins with the law. The first occasion was when he was enjoying a ride on his motorbike early one morning in London.

'I couldn't resist accelerating away from this patrol car,' he recalls. 'It was a beautiful day and the streets were empty. But the police were much faster than I thought and round the next corner they caught up with me. One copper got out and gave me a really comprehensive telling-off, which I admit I richly deserved.

'The other occasion when I crossed swords with the police was rather more worrying. I was driving down the motorway and this police Range Rover followed me for miles. Eventually he pulled me up and I thought I was really in trouble. But the only thing he wanted was my autograph!'

Good health and fitness are another subject very close to Martin's heart – 'The things I won't allow myself are ill-health, lethargy and fatigue,' he says – and to this end he follows a strict diet, is a teetotaller, and likes to work out in the 'fitness room' in the four-floor Victorian villa in North London where he lives when not playing *The Chief*. It is here at home, too, that he can dispense with the power-dressing required by his role and revert to his normal old jeans and trainers – a style he refers to as 'very casual and wild – gross *déshabillé*, in fact.'

'As an actor it's important to get in training when you know you have a busy time ahead,' he says. 'I'm not one of those glistening people in a vest, but I am into personal fitness – cardiovascular and stretching stuff. I have to confess that it's only if I know I'm going to have to take my shirt off that I'll go and work out at a gym – and then it's strictly for vanity's sake.'

Martin is also an enthusiastic supporter of Chinese medicine techniques as well as being a strong advocate for the vegan diet. He stopped eating meat as long ago as 1971 – long before it was fashionable – and now follows a diet which excludes anything that comes from animals.

'Sometimes people ask me what I eat. Which always puzzles me. I eat very well because there are plenty of substitutes for meat and dairy products. I never feel I go without.'

He believes that taking herbal remedies and using techniques like acupuncture are a much better and more natural way of taking care of the body than waiting until things go wrong and then

*Cade always likes to be at the heart of the action, here he is keeping an eye on events while his men search a stretch of river for a body.*

swallowing handfuls of manufactured prescribed drugs.

'I also take supplements like ginseng and evening primrose, on a regular basis,' he adds. 'It's difficult to analyse what they have, but they definitely give me a general feeling of well-being and metabolic ease. And mentally it's good to know that everything I am putting into my body will harmonize.'

Listening to Martin talking about health and fitness, it comes as something of a surprise to learn that one of his favourite episodes in *The Chief* was about drugs and that he shares the view that Cade expressed in the story that they should be legalized.

'It was a radical move and one bound to stir up controversy,' he reflects. 'Decriminalizing certain drugs in order to take them from the criminal element is something that is close to my own views. People will always take drugs and they will pay whatever you charge, and then it becomes adulterated and they mix poison with it and still charge the same amount. If it was legal and controlled there would be controls over quantity and quality.

'Cade himself used the parallel of prohibition in the twenties and thirties when they prohibited alcohol and handed it straight to the Mafia. I rather think that is what we are doing with drugs.'

Martin admits candidly that he did experiment himself when he was younger. 'I have been through all that sixties stuff, a bit of innocent joint-smoking like most people of my age. Now I have gone beyond it. It was a useful time, it was something that opened different areas of the mind and different areas of society.

'Legalizing drugs isn't a laissez-faire idea – it is not so that everybody can go and kill themselves and show their children how to do it. There should be adequate control and very, very responsible rules. But you have to take this thing out of the hands of the drug barons. And for things like drink-driving, they should bring in stricter watchdogs and impose higher penalties.'

As a non-drinker himself, Martin knows he can easily be described as a kill-joy; and where decriminalizing drugs is concerned he feels people are more worried about the symbolism of such an action rather than the practicalities.

Though he is happy to be quoted publicly on such matters, he is just as fiercely determined to guard his private life in London – where he lives with his partner, Vicki Kimm, a television presenter – or at the isolated crofter's cottage that he recently bought on the Scottish borders.

'The cottage is an essential part of my life. It's in the middle of a wilderness, at the end of a two-mile unmade road – a bit like a drawbridge. It takes people so long to drive I can spot who's coming long before they arrive – and take evasive action if necessary.'

He does, though, remain in close touch with his three children from his first marriage to actress Jill Allen – sons Luke (23) and Joe (20) and daughter, Sophie (18) all of whom want to follow in their father's footsteps. 'There is quite a Shaw dynasty,' he laughs – though he has warned them all about the difficulties of the profession and underlined his conviction that professional satisfaction means more than fame and fortune.

'There are some aspects of wealth that'd be wonderful,' he says. 'But I don't believe in fame, it's ephemeral. I don't enjoy being stared at and pestered. I feel hijacked and de-personalized.

'One of the reasons that I love this job so much is because the production team have respect for all my 30 years of experience. Thanks to their enthusiasm and the scripts I have been able to create someone who has forcefulness, drive and charisma, but the mind of a philosopher. I don't think there is anything like it on the screen.'

And the future for him after the fifth series of *The Chief*?

'Cade is in a really tight spot at the end of the last episode,' Martin says with one of his most enigmatic smiles. 'His future is very much in the balance. So who knows what the future holds for him – or for me, for that matter? But that's how we both like it – taking risks . . . '

# 7

# AIRBORN WITH THE CHIEF

Whenever the weather is good and he has time off from filming *The Chief*, Martin Shaw heads straight for the small private airfield at Swanton Morley just outside East Dereham and takes off in his own aircraft into the skies of East Anglia. Flying a couple of thousand feet above the countryside he can get a pilot's eye view of the area that he also knows as Eastland and of which he is the Chief Constable. It is a unique experience that few other actors can have shared.

Once at the controls of his single-engined aircraft, Martin has the wide skies of Norfolk to choose from. He can fly to The Wash – to the west of Swanton Morley – or, by going east, cross the Norfolk Broads and head over the North Sea. To the south lie the busier air traffic lanes of Suffolk and Essex which he prefers to fly in only when he has plenty of time on his hands.

The freedom of flying is one that Martin relishes as an opportunity to escape from the demands of his busy life. Flying also represents the fulfilment of a dream he has had since childhood – and it is a subject that he talks about with undisguised pleasure. Indeed, close observers of the TV series may well have spotted that the Chief wears a tie-clip featuring a tiny vintage aircraft, while Cade's home is filled with flying paraphernalia.

Martin's flying has not, however, been without its moments of incident and drama, as he recalls with the kind of wry smile common to virtually every amateur pilot . . .

'I had this dream that I wanted to fly ever since I was five years old,' he says. 'I got my first chance about fifteen years ago when I appeared on the BBC programme *A Sporting Chance* where they taught me to fly a glider. From that moment on I was just itching for the chance to fly a light aircraft and get my pilot's licence. The role of the Chief at last gave me the opportunity I wanted.'

Even before he had been introduced in the third series, Martin was living at Watton and had found his way to the nearest airfield a couple of miles down the road at Shipdham. Here he enrolled for

the tough course of lessons with an instructor that every would-be pilot must undertake.

As an amateur pilot myself, I know just how demanding the lessons can be and how exhilarating the day is when you are finally allowed to fly solo for the first time. Martin tackled the course with enormous enthusiasm – though, as a member of *The Chief*'s production team was to tell me, there were worries about him flying and the additional costs that this added to the series' insurance premium against the loss of their star. The man himself, quite oblivious to all this, completed the course during his second summer of filming and was awarded his pilots' licence. 'I felt an enormous sense of achievement getting that licence,' he smiles at the memory.

Martin's joy was almost turned into a nightmare on his very first flight from Shipdham with a passenger. Indeed, he needed every bit of the training he had been given in order to make an unexpected emergency landing. Not surprisingly, he recalls the events very clearly.

'I was flying a single-engined Piper Cub,' he says. 'And the passenger was my brother, Jeremy. I had taken him up for a flight around the Norfolk coast. On the return journey the engine suddenly quit as I was approaching the airfield. I didn't know it at the time but the plane had suffered a major fuel leak in the carburettor. It meant I had to make an emergency landing called a

*Martin Shaw's great passion is flying, a hobby he has also been able to introduce into The Chief.*

'Dead Stick' landing without the engine on which can be very dangerous.

'Any engine failure is frightening, but 90 percent of the time you can get the plane down safely. It is one of the things you have to do during the very intensive training course for a licence and I had done it lots of times before. Norfolk is very flat and my instructor had shut the engine down on several occasions and asked me to deal with it.

'This time, though, I was the only pilot on board! It was a very rare thing to have happened – it only occurs about once in a million flights – but it was very unfair to have happened to me on my first flight. But I was approaching my own airfield and knew I just had to go through the procedures I'd been taught. If it had been anything other than an engine failure – such as a part of the plane falling off – then I would have been very frightened indeed. So I went ahead and made the ''Dead Stick'' landing and got down quite safely.

'I was really pleased,' adds Martin. 'I've flown lots of times since and what happened encouraged me because I realized I could cope in an emergency. My brother Jeremy didn't know anything was wrong until the sudden descent to earth. Funnily, though, he hasn't flown with me since!'

Martin's interest in flying also helped solve one problem the production team were having when he joined the series: what the Chief did in his admittedly limited spare time.

'Alan Cade needed a hobby,' he recalls, 'so I suggested flying which seemed a bit more likely thing for him than golf or bridge. The producer and the director loved the idea and that's how Cade's flat came to be filled with things associated with flying.'

Martin was able to get behind the controls of a plane on camera in the final episode of the fourth series in which Peter Egan appeared as a suave businessman, Simon Duval, who was trying to poach officers from the Eastland Police Force for his own private security firm. Cade met Duval when he flew his plane into a local airfield to discuss setting up a joint force of security men, immigration officers and Eastland Police in order to catch a gang of illegal immigrants. It was an operation that was destined to turn sour when one of the workers died while struggling to escape.

'I would certainly like it if the Chief could fly a bit more in the series,' Martin says, 'but in any event I plan to grab any opportunities to get aloft whenever time permits.'

There seems no doubt that the aeronautical drama Martin Shaw has experienced both on and off the screen has only served to increase his enthusiasm for flying. Now with a licence and his own aircraft the skies of Eastland are indeed his . . .

*Cade flew to a meeting with sauve businessman, Simon Duval (Peter Egan), which was to have far-reaching implications for both him and his force.*

# 8

# THE CHIEF'S PEOPLE:
# Part Two

## Series 3-5

### THE TOUGH CRIME-BUSTER
### Head of CID Sean McCloud (Stuart McGugan)

Sean McCloud, Cade's first appointment as his boss of Eastland's CID, was a fiery, rough diamond who had made it to the top ranks of the police force despite – or perhaps even because of – his working class background and a career beset with personal problems. He did, though, become the man whom the Chief turned to when he wanted an honest answer as his radical policing made him an increasingly isolated figure.

The role of McCloud, which was specially developed by Ray Jenkins as a foil for Alan Cade, fitted the Scottish actor, Stuart McGugan, like a glove – all the more so due to his long experience in the theatre and a whole swathe of law and order television series such as *Taggart*, *Spender* and *The Bill*.

'McCloud was certainly seen as a hard man,' reflects Stuart McGugan in his familiar deep Scottish brogue, 'but I added bits and pieces to his character as we went along so that finally he became a man you sensed had a lot of common sense and had also seen it and done it before. There was certainly a rough, tough edge to him, but he enjoyed being taken into the Chief's confidence – even if he didn't always agree with his boss.'

To his job as the head of CID, McCloud brought a lifetime spent dealing with the underside of life which had started for him in childhood growing up in an impoverished Presbyterian background. A combination of sheer hard work, a fair bit of bloodymindedness and the occasional resort to some of the less traditional methods of villain catching, had enabled Sean to make it to the top as Chief Superintendent as Strathclyde CID before his promotion to Eastland.

However, the personal cost had been high. For years, McCloud had battled with a drink problem which proved one of the factors in the breakdown of his marriage. But he had faced this crisis with the same single-minded resolution that was the hallmark of his police work: he joined Alcoholics Anonymous and by the time he was recruited to Cade's force he had been a teetotaller for five years.

Stuart McGugan, an actor of considerable presence and gritty charm, quickly succeeded in making McCloud the kind of hard-nosed detective beloved by many viewers. Indeed, his career has been a rich mixture of roles from his days as a trainee at the Royal Scottish Academy of Dramatic Art by way of seasons at Leeds, Canterbury, Newcastle, and The Royal Shakespeare Company at Stratford-on-Avon as well as a period across the Atlantic appearing with the American Conservatory Theatre in San Francisco.

On television, however, he came to public notice in the long-lasting BBC comedy series about a British Army concert party in Bombay, *It Ain't Half Hot, Mum* (1973-81). It was here that he first worked for director David Croft, who also cast him again in the recent equally successful series about life butlering for the upper classes, *You Rang My Lord?* In the interim, Stuart has also appeared in *The Brief* which John Frankau directed; the horror series, *Beasts*, written by Nigel 'Quartermass' Kneale; and the musical *Tutti Frutti* directed by Tony Smith for the BBC in 1986.

Being signed by Anglia for *The Chief* brought back memories for Stuart of filming one particular episode of *It Ain't Half Hot, Mum* In October 1973.

'The Beeb sent us up to Norfolk to film this sequence supposedly set in a steamy jungle' he says. 'To make a clear-running stream look like a misty Indian swamp they stirred up the mud and dunked dry ice in it. They also took along two crocodiles – one obviously fake and the other actually quite frightningly realistic – and a whole collection of BBC potted plants.

'Later on the screen the jungle looked quite impenetrable and sweaty, but I can assure you that it was actually freezing cold. And all the sweat on our faces as we hopped in and out of the swamp was glycerine!'

Filming *The Chief* proved to be rather more comfortable if no less exhilarating for Stuart when he joined in the third series.

The elements of the tough Scot's character that appealed to Cade were immediately apparent: they shared the same unbending hatred for even the slightest whiff of corruption and both were men who could instinctively sense prejudices in those above and below them. Both also jealously guarded their right to lives of their own.

'McCloud was a man I could really relate to,' Stuart says. 'I know from my own upbringing in Scotland that there are people like him who sacrifice everything for their jobs and lose their families in the process. They are obsessive about work and take to drink to get a little respite from what drives them on. But when they come to terms with themselves and their problems they are just the sort of men you want on your side.

'What Cade needed when McCloud joined him was an ally. The Chief obviously wasn't going to get on with Anne Stewart and was becoming increasingly isolated. So he had to have someone to talk to, and this provided the interplay between Cade and McCloud. He was the man to back up the Chief. In time, of course, being the sort of men they were was bound to lead to disagreements.'

Indeed, McCloud's single-minded pursuit of the truth eventually lead him to become increasingly frustrated with the letter of the law when he found it hampering rather helping his cases. Nowhere was this better illustrated than in the fourth series when one case after another of his began to fail because evidence was considered to be 'inadmissable'.

'This made McCloud decide to take matters into his own hands,' Stuart goes on. 'He allowed a file containing the clear evidence against a child murderer who had been acquitted to be leaked to the press. Cade was furious about this and it cost McCloud his promotion to ACC Ops.'

From that moment on, the fiery Scot's career in the Eastland Force was obviously coming to an end – especially with the appointment of a new ACC Ops, David Kendal (Simon Slater) which effectively put him out of the important decision making. The conclusion of series four saw the end of Stuart McGugan's contribution to *The Chief*.

*McCloud on a mission with other members of the Eastland Force.*

Brenda Reid explains: 'It is hard to keep coming up with new stories for Cade's deputies and close associates, and I think time just ran out for McCloud. But Stuart was another of the highly accomplished actors who have made an important contribution to the success of the series.'

# THE CONVENTIONAL POLICEMAN

## Deputy Chief Constable Wes Morton (Bosco Hogan)

DCC Wesley Morton, Cade's new right-hand man, has a strikingly different personality to that of his boss. A sound, very conventional policeman by nature, he does have the same honesty and driving ambition to serve the public but shares none of the Chief's love of controversy and risk-taking.

For the Irish actor Bosco Hogan playing this senior officer who runs his life by the book has meant being reunited with John Davies who directed him in Anglia's six-part P D James thriller, *A Taste For Death*, made in 1988.

'I was delighted when John rang me in Dublin and asked if I would appear in *The Chief*,' Bosco says, 'but I have to be honest and admit that because I'm not a great television watcher I didn't know a great deal about the series before I joined. But thanks to all the help I've had from everyone on the team, especially John Alderson who is an absolute walking encyclopedia on the police, I'm really enjoying the experience.'

Despite a long career in both the theatre and on television, the role of DCC Morton is the first policeman that Bosco has played. Already, though, he shows every indication of having got under the skin of the tall, balding rather austere policeman whose career has been built on the great traditions of the force.

'Morton is actually rather right wing in his views which makes for the interesting occasional clash with Cade who is much more liberal,' explains Bosco. 'They don't quite see eye to eye on certain things. Where Cade would be inclined to take the liberal line, Morton would want to go in there and be much more severe and strict.

'He is in fact, I think, a good old fashioned copper. He is inclined to go along the traditional lines. Possibly because he is inclined to believe that is the right thing to do anyway, but also with an eye to keeping his career options fully open.'

Bosco, who was born and raised in Dublin, has also kept his own career options open over the years by working in the widest possible range of productions from Shakespeare to contemporary dramas and serials. He began with the famous Abbey Theatre in Dublin where he received excellent reviews for his roles as Stephen

Dedalus in *Ulysses in Nighttown* and M Duclos in *Hotel Paradiso*. He also appeared in several productions at Dublin's Gate Theatre – notably in the *Threepenny Opera* and *Heartbreak House* – before deciding to try his luck in London.

'The move got me into television,' he recalls, 'where I did a lot of things including Jonathan Harker in *Count Dracula* for BBC TV and Frederick, Duke of York in another of their productions, *Prince Regent*. My first work for Anglia was actually *Miss Morrison's Ghosts*, a story of parapsychology with Hannah Gordon and Dame Wendy Hillier. I also did a couple of *Tales of the Unexpected* and then the P D James with John Davies.'

Bosco has also appeared in several films including John Boorman's *Zardoz* in which he played George Saden, and the Walt Disney production, *Race for Survival*, where he had the starring role of Paul Garrison. He also reprised the role of Stephen Dadalus in the cinema version of *A Portrait of the Artist as a Young Man*.

After seven years living away from his native Ireland, Bosco decided to return home to Dublin – 'because I didn't want to bring my family up in London.' Since then his work has often required him to travel outside the country on assignments such as *The Chief*.

Although the earlier career of DCC Wes Morton before he came to Eastland is sketchy, according to Bosco, he is a 'solid, but hungry' policeman who learned about the importance of honour and duty from several 'old school' coppers who very much shaped his character. He thinks that time is a precious commodity and should be used wisely, and has no sympathy for those who show any inclination to be 'soft on crime'. Morton is ambitious to climb higher in the force but will always play a safer game to get there.

'Although Morton will ask Cade direct questions, he is always slightly formal with him,' Bosco explains. 'He can feel peeved at some of the Chief's decisions and is suspicious of new ideas. I don't think he and Cade would be friends by any means, but they do have a respect for each other.'

Like Martin Shaw, Bosco is a fitness enthusiast and makes a point of going running every day before beginning work. He also likes to play squash, tennis and go on cycle rides. He is a keen horseman, too.

One of Bosco's skills as an actor is a mastery of accents which has earned him a lot of work on the RTE Radio Repertory Company in Ireland and BBC Radio. He is also something of a handyman, being good at carpentry, plumbing and car maintenance. He does not expect to put these to use on *The Chief*.

'I'm going to have to invent quite a lot of Morton's past to make sense of some of his actions,' says Bosco, 'but that is the sort of challenge any actor relishes when developing a new character. There is no doubt that Morton is a bit intimidated by the Home Office people, and dislikes interference from outside the force. He is certainly alarmed by Cade's ability to strike out on his own and defy the Establishment.

'I don't think he likes sticking his neck out, he's much happier working by the book. In other words, he's the kind of man a lot of members of the public see as the very backbone of the police force.'

With the pressure mounting on Cade throughout the fifth series, Morton also begins to start questioning himself about just how far he can go in supporting *The Chief*.

'That is going to be his dilemma,' adds Bosco with a smile, 'and how it works out is up to the scriptwriters. As any actors will tell you, I just have to wait for each script and see!'

## THE GREAT PEOPLE-MOTIVATOR

### Detective Superintendent Rose Penfold (Gillian Bevan)

The new, ambitious Head of Eastland CID, Rose Penfold, is also being played by an actress who has not previously appeared in a crime or detective series. However, Gillian Bevan was a fan of *The Chief* and watched a few of the early episodes with Tim Pigott-Smith and became a regular viewer when Martin Shaw took on the leading role.

'I think Martin is a terrific actor,' the vivacious brunette says, 'and the chance to work with him was just too good to miss. The fact that Rose and Alan Cade have such a good working relationship is an added bonus. And whereas the Chief had doubts about Anne Stewart's potential, he has no such misgivings about Rose.'

DS Penfold, who is a quick-witted and intuitive policewoman with a nose for getting to the facts, has benefited from the slowly changing attitudes towards high ranking women officers in the police force and reached her present position through a lot of hard and often dangerous work. She has also worked with Cade before.

'They were together in London for a time,' Gillian explains. 'She worked with him in charge of firearms and drugs. So she knows all about his attitudes towards such things and his reputation for getting things done in the face of interference and even opposition.'

One of the elements about Rose that particularly appealed to her when she was offered the role was a chance to play herself.

'I've never played anybody contemporary on television before,' she confesses. 'I've done a lot of character parts putting on wigs and make-up and using silly voices, so it is nice to be playing someone who is similar to me and also to get into some decent clothes!'

Despite her position, Rose does not have to wear a uniform and hopes this will give her the chance to dress fashionably, though not provocatively. She is also the only senior member of Cade's team at the moment who does not have her own office.

Gillian's slightly disparaging description of her earlier roles gives little clue to the variety of her work on both the stage and TV screen. Born in Stockport, Cheshire, she followed her childhood ambition to be an actress by training at the Central School of Speech and Drama. Then followed the hard slog through repertory theatres in Perth, Salisbury and Farnham before getting her first major roles at the Bristol Old Vic. Her breakthrough to public recognition came when she joined Alan Ayckbourn's theatre in Scarborough and for three years appeared in some of his most successful plays.

In London she has since combined appearances in West End productions such as *Follies* with more traditional roles for the Royal Shakespeare Company in *As You Like It* (as Celia) and *The Wizard of Oz* (playing Dorothy). On television she has been seen in BBC's *Ghostwatch*, *Never the Twain* for Thames TV and Granada's prestigious version of JB Priestley's *Lost Empires* where she worked with Lord Olivier on what was to prove one of his last appearances. She came to *The Chief* from the comedy role of Vanda in the series about a bakery, *All Night Long*, starring Keith Barron.

'I did a lot of reading about life in the police force when I was offered the role,' she says. 'I also spent time with John Alderson and with a very high ranking female police officer at the Home Office. She was a fund of information and very good at confirming some of my theories about how women operate in a man's world. I thought it was very important to get the look of my character exactly right.

'My instinct told me I needed to have costumes that didn't provoke comments and yet still had an air of authority about them. My adviser told me that being a woman in the police she had had to think much more about the effect of what she looked like and how she behaved towards others – in particular towards male officers.

'The alternatives for a woman trying to make a career in the police are not many. In fact, it's a case of "You're damned if you do and damned if you don't." You can either be one of the lads and drink pints of beer and therefore risk being labelled a bit of a slag or otherwise you're labelled stand-offish if you don't go to the pub. To give you an example, I heard about this female police officer who decided to be one of the lads until she was promoted to Sergeant and then had to actively stop that 'canteen culture' thing and re-invent herself, if you like, and be very careful about what she was doing and wearing so that she could command respect.'

Gillian's research ultimately gave her a clear idea of Rose's place in the Chief's heirarchy.

'Rose has actually gone through that process of learning and sorted it all out. She is now accepted on her own terms and has gained the right to be treated as a professional. She may be a woman in a man's world, but she is there on her own terms. And she's got enough people skills to be able to cope with that.'

'People skills' is, in fact, a favourite expression of Gillian's in referring to her character's abilities.

'The production people didn't want to make Rose overly tough or even suggest there might be an element of lesbianism in her. She is personable and able to hold her own. But the real skill she has is that she can still keep hold of her femininity when dealing with people. So she commands the respect and yet has got the best of both worlds. But she must never stifle that femininity too much, which is a tricky thing.'

Rose Penfold has, in fact, a husband, Michael (played by Martin Troakes) who had wanted to be a policeman, but because of bad eyesight has had to settle for a civilian job in the force. He would like to start a family, but she has gone past that. This, Gillian says, has lead to a certain conflict between them when Michael realizes just what a high-flyer his wife has become.

Gillian has found the happy atmosphere of filming *The Chief* very conducive to putting in a good performance and gives her plenty of opportunity for both serious and light-hearted moments.

'It's just great fun to do,' she smiles enthusiastically. 'I get to order about lots of young men in uniform. They have to call me, "Ma'am", and stand up when I come into the room. So in that respect it's great to be a woman in a position of power!'

How does she see the relationship between Rose and the Chief?

'It is so rare to see two people at that level having a working relationship who actually like and respect each other. And there is no hint of anything else going on. Cade is a bit of a one-off and I think that is why he is attracted to Rose in a working situation because she is also at his level and brings a different logic and a different way of looking at situations. I think they feel quite sympatico.'

The relationship between her and Wes Morton is, she thinks, rather more tricky.

'Rose is walking a fine line with Morton. She has to work very closely with him and there are times when Cade will ask her opinion instead of Morton's – and that is a sensitive area. But because she is a great people motivator she works very hard at making herself "user-friendly" towards him. Not a threat. That's her great skill: people prefer to have her as an ally rather than make an enemy of her.'

Gillian has no doubt that DS Rose Penfold is highly ambitious.

'I think she is aiming for the top,' she says. 'Cade certainly thinks she is top potential. He wants her to be his staff officer because in this way she can get a greater insight into how the role of being the Chief pans out. She is definitely on a roll now because Cade has given her the confidence to believe that it is possible.

'My adviser at the Home Office felt that there were now enough young people at her level setting an example for the younger generation to believe, "We can go for it" that they will break the mould. We've had a woman prime minister and at some stage there is going to be a woman Chief Constable, of that I'm sure.'

Another significant development she heard about at this same time further underlined her conviction.

'There was a senior policewoman who was seven months pregnant and still going about her job dealing with the public, setting up conferences and such like. My adviser was thrilled to think that here was a woman who had the courage to believe that it was possible for someone with a high ranking police career to also have babies at the same time.'

As Gillian has committed herself to the future of *The Chief*, she also nurses ambitions that maybe where Karen Archer was denied the chance of the top postion she might succeed. 'But Rose is faced with the same thing as any woman in a male-dominated enclave – she just needs to keep battering away.'

But could she see herself as a policewoman?

'When I was talking to that friend at the Home Office I realized what huge sacrifices she had had to make to get where she was and I think that is the tragedy. Certainly, things are changing in the police, but the fallout of women is so high because it is such hard work and the hours are so uncivilized in terms of being able to fulfill any kind of outside life as well. So I suppose the simple answer is No!' Gillian believes there is great scope for Rose.

'I love the part and it's also true that there just aren't that many good ones around for women, especially parts that have a new angle on a theme. I feel quite partisan towards Rose and so I am just gently trying to remind the writers that the subjects of racism and sexism can't be dealt with in one episode as they are actually endemic within the whole structure of policing. They are areas that interest a lot of people, too, and I think *The Chief* could make some valuable statements. After all, the series has quite a reputation for being ahead of the news, doesn't it?'

# THE AMBASSADOR OF LOVE

## Marie-Pierre Arnoux (Juliette Mole)

There was something almost inevitable about Alan Cade's first serious romantic involvement being with a chic and pretty Frenchwoman. As a student in Paris in 1968 he had, after all, met and fallen in love with a young girl, Yvonne, by whom he had had a love child. Although this relationship had eventually failed, the Paris of lovers was never far from his thoughts, and his attraction to the French Embassy attacheü Marie-Pierre Arnoux was somehow a matter of fate.

Behind the scenes, the love match had a rather more practical objective, however, according to Ruth Boswell. 'We thought it was a good idea that Cade had a French girlfriend in case we had been able to take the series into Europe. In fact, we had a number of storylines in which we could have used her to give a more European dimension to the series, but the economics defeated us.'

Although Marie-Pierre was therefore fated to make only a short-lived appearance in the series, she made a strong impact on the new Chief and viewers alike. As a woman she was very different from Cade's first Parisian lover, Yvonne. Single-minded about pursuing her career in the diplomatic service, she was not so blinded by love as to be willing to give up her independence for the equally dedicated Cade – a factor which made their relationship one as fraught with tension as it was with passion. The demands of their respective careers often kept them apart for long periods of time, putting an added strain on the affair.

Juliette Mole, a lovely brunette in her thirties, brought to the role of Marie-Pierre the advantages of being half-French, plus the expertise of a dual career as an artist and interior decorator and that of an actress. It comes as no real surprise to learn that Juliette says she earns far more from her artistic endeavours than from acting – but admits she has had the urge to act since her childhood and can never resist the call of the camera.

'My mother was French,' she explains, 'and although I was born in London I went to the Lycée Français where I studied art and languages and got my first experience of acting. I think it has been a great help to my career that I can speak six languages.

'I've been working as an artist for about seven years now, which keeps me busy when I'm not filming. I paint anything: pictures, walls, fabrics. For instance, I recently had a big job in New York at Bianca Jagger's boyfriend's house. I did a mural in the hallway of a ruin with broken stone and was there for two weeks. In fact, I've worked for a lot of very rich people – they are the only ones who can afford me because I am very expensive. I charge vast amounts of money – thousands of pounds!'

Juliette smiles without a trace of false modesty – her full order book demonstrating more eloquently than any words the demand for her artistic talent. Why, then, act for so much less?

'Because I love acting and filming *The Chief* in particular was such good fun,' she says.

Prior to the Anglia series she had appeared in two other top crime series – both based on the works of her favourite detective story writer, Agatha Christie – *Poirot* and *Miss Marple*. Neither of these series were, though, her first introduction to the law. This occurred in real life when she was living on a houseboat moored on the River Thames at Chelsea.

It was while following this taste for an unusual lifestyle that she also met her husband, Lloyd, with whom she now shares a long-distance relationship not unlike that which she had with Alan Cade.

'I lived on my houseboat, the Patriach, for six years and it was great fun,' she recalls. 'The river police sometimes used to pop in for tea and they once gave me a ride in their patrol boat. I suppose it might seem like a kind of omen. It was also while I was on the boat that I met my husband, Lloyd Owen. We shared the same mooring and I just got talking to him. I thought he was very good looking as he has very blue eyes and our romance just developed from there.'

Lloyd, the son of Glyn Owen who played the combative Jack Rolfe in the long-running TV series, *Howard's Way*, is an actor, too, and has recently spent two years in Europe filming *The Young Indiana Jones Chronicles* as Indiana's father. The couple were married in 1990 and moved on to dry land and a flat in Battersea when their son, Maxim, was born a year later. Juliette, though, still hankers after the life on the water and says the couple plan to buy another houseboat soon.

Of her role as Cade's first screen girlfriend she says, 'It was tailor-made for me because I am half French. I did have to do my homework to find out all about the life of a French Embassy attaché, but it was a good part and I was sorry when they decided to write me out of the series.

'Marie-Pierre had to make a choice between Cade or her career and she decided her work came first. So she went off to Tokyo and left Cade absolutely devastated. The parting seemed to have quite an effect on viewers, too.

'But I still have plenty of happy memories of the series. Martin Shaw was a lovely man to work with and he really understands women. He is very comfortable in their presence. I was not at all surprised when they soon had someone else in my place in the Chief's affections . . .'

# THE BEGUILING IMAGE-MAKER

## Alison Dell (Ingrid Lacey)

Although Alan Cade was undoubtedly still hurting inside from the failure of his romance with Marie-Pierre Arnoux, three episodes after her departure for Japan a new woman walked into his life in the shape of lively, blonde public relations consultant, Alison Dell. Not one to mix words, she told the Chief that his image was in need of improvement. A public opinion poll conducted in Eastland had revealed that he was unpopular and his style of leadership had failed to reassure local people that he could successfully control the region's crime.

Such strong words hardly pleased Cade. But always the realist – and impressed by Alison's style and determination – he agreed to employ her to improve this jaundiced view and at the same time provide him with feedback on the public's attitude towards the working of his force. It was a decision that had far-reaching effects for him publicly and privately when the couple's working relationship soon spilled over into their off-duty lives . . .

Few actresses could have come better qualified for the role of Alison than 34-year-old Ingrid Lacey who has not only worked as a secretary in three London police stations, but when she is in between assignments runs her own PR company advising businessmen on the best way of presenting and promoting their services.

Ingrid Lacey, however, says that in real life she is actually not at all like Alison.

'Of course, as an actress I have had to mix with a lot of PR Officers,' she admits, 'but Alison Dell is not operating in the cut and thrust of show business. She is a gentle character working on business contracts. I certainly didn't base her on someone like the dynamic showbusiness PR Officer, Lynne Franks.'

In fact, Ingrid has made a habit throughout her acting career of avoiding parts that are in any way like herself. 'I prefer being in other people's shoes. That is what attracted me to acting in the first place – pretending to be someone else.'

Ingrid trained for her career at the Bristol Old Vic Theatre School and then worked in a variety of roles on the stage and screen. On TV she played the British agent Alice Kavanagh in the spy thriller, *Saracen*; was the librarian girlfriend of George (Glen Murphy) in the popular series about firemen, *London's Burning*; and was the outrageous man-eater Helen who cavorted around a bedroom in suspenders with her lover in *A Woman's Guide to Adultery*. She is, though, perhaps best known to viewers for her role as the lesbian news editor – also called Helen – in the award-winning Channel 4 comedy series, *Drop the Dead Donkey*.

'Helen in *A Woman's Guide to Adultery* was a mega-monster which was great fun to act and very different from Helen in *Drop The Dead Donkey*,' she says. 'But Alison Dell was nothing like either of them – and none of the characters are like me. I have considerably less get up and go than Helen in *A Woman's Guide to Adultery*, but a bit more emotion than Alison in *The Chief*.

This notoriety was, however, a long way in the future when Ingrid had her spell working for the police and later set up her training company.

'When I was an out of work actress, I temped for the police at Stoke Newington, Dalston and Kentish Town police stations,' she recalls, 'so you can't get much more street cred than that. I was doing secretarial back-up work, typing statements, that kind of thing. It was as good a way as any of getting a real insight into what is going on in the police because I was handling all their correspondence and paperwork.'

And her experience of public relations? 'I run a training company called Face to Face. It is not strictly PR, but we advise people on how to handle problems with the way they present their business, and how to get across their ideas. I have worked with a lot of big companies on the sort of image things that faced the Chief, so it was not an area that was unfamiliar to me.'

During her appearances in the third series Alison did not take long to impress Cade with her skill. He was also obviously taken by her beauty and unspoilt charm. But there was one big drawback.

'Alison had pushed very hard to get the job with Eastland Police,' Ingrid reminisces, 'and she and Cade got on very well. Indeed, that was the hallmark of their relationship – they were very friendly and affectionate. They looked like the ideal couple, the sort of whom you think, ''Why on earth can't they get it together?'' But Cade was still smarting from his affair with Marie-Pierre. And they both of them had busy lives which put a lot of pressure on them. The truth was that neither of them was really ready to commit.'

And so the affair between the Chief and the PR consultant faded out just as the one with Marie-Pierre had done because of a lack of commitment. Ingrid, though, would have very much liked the scriptwriters to have kept the affair going.

'Looking back now,' she reflects, 'I think Alison should have tried harder to win Cade. I would have gone after him. You think to yourself, ''Oh, come on, he's very attractive, you'll not do better in Norfolk. Get in there girl.'' So you can see I really am not at *all* like Alison Dell!'

# THE MAVERICK BARRISTER

## Gemma Marshall (Maureen Beattie)

The outspoken, left-wing lawyer Gemma Marshall, who made her appearance in the fourth series and became a focal point of several episodes, was by no stretch of the imagination another of 'Cade's Women', as some of the newspaper reports heralding her arrival wanted to paint her. But there was certainly a twinkle in her eye for the Chief whenever their paths crossed – a twinkle that Cade was unable to resist returning, sensing a forthright personality as single-minded and determined as his own.

Actress Maureen Beattie with her piercing green eyes which are, in fact, as hard to avoid off screen as on, came to the role fresh from starring in 29 episodes of the long-running BBC series, *Casualty*, which had made her a household name. But once she had exchanged her nurse's uniform for a barrister's wig and gown any fears of type-casting immediately disappeared.

Just as she had done for her role in *Casualty*, Maureen researched the part of Gemma Marshall with painstaking care and from her enquiries she says she learned enough secrets of the legal profession to make Gemma Marshall every bit as much of a rebel as the Chief himself.

'I jumped at the opportunity of playing Gemma,' Maureen says, her voice switching easily from her natural, gentle Scottish lilt into the more direct and precise tones of a lawyer. 'She was fiery, controversial and with a strong sense of right and wrong. You could describe her as a real maverick where the law is concerned.

'Before I started filming *The Chief*, I spent a lot of time watching barristers at work at the Old Bailey. I also had a number of lengthy discussions with a woman barrister in her chambers. She gave me hints on what to wear and how to conduct myself when cross-examining a witness.

'I found the whole place fascinating and came away full of admiration for the profession. What barristers basically do is act – which is what I attempt to do. They are also highly intelligent, sharp and quick witted. These were all the qualities I tried to bring to Gemma right from the beginning when I appeared to defend a father accused of murdering his baby daughter.'

Maureen's own sense of dedication to her craft was sown in childhood: her father was a popular comedian and her mother ran a modelling agency. Although she was actually born in Donegal, she and the family moved to Glasgow when she was still a baby. She grew up with showbusiness in her blood.

'My father, Johnnie Beattie, was well-known on the Scottish club circuit,' she says, 'and my friends expected Dad to be cracking jokes all the time. But to us that was just what he did for a living. Mum ran a model agency – and that was glamorous, too – but we just looked on it all as the norm.'

To begin with it seemed that Marueen's own life would follow a kind of 'norm', too, although thanks to her father she appeared as a child actor on several programmes for Scottish Television. When she left school, however, she opted to work as a laboratory technician in Glasgow.

But the allure of showbusiness with its mixture of delights and pitfalls gradually grew more attractive than labouring over test tubes and so Maureen signed up at the Royal Scottish Academy of Music and Dramatic Art. After gaining her Equity card she followed for a time in her father's footsteps working as a comedy feed on the tough Scottish variety circuit. It was to be an experience she would never forget.

Hardened by the demands of live performance, Maureen then embarked on a series of stage and television roles which have since made her so popular with casting directors and producers – not the least of them *The Chief*'s Brenda Reid and Ruth Boswell. Among her television roles have been parts in *The Lost Tribe, Hard to Get, Should We Come Back Tomorrow?, Troubles and Strife* and the long-running Scottish TV police series, *Taggart*.

It was in *Casualty*, however, that she became a national favourite playing the tough Scottish staff nurse, Sandra Nicholl. Her early experiences of medicine in the laboratory and her well-honed professionalism enabled her to turn the nurse into something of a popular icon. But after several years at Holby General Hospital, she thought it was time for a change.

'Leaving *Casualty* was not an easy decision,' she admits today, 'and it took some time for me to make. It was a wonderful programme and I had some great storylines. But I just thought I couldn't get any better so it was time for me to go. I knew if I had stayed for another series I would have been there until it finished.'

Her first roles after leaving *Casualty* could not have been more different. On television she played the snobbish daughter of a Scottish highlander and his cancer-stricken wife in *The Long Roads* for the BBC in 1993 (interestingly, with her younger sister, Louise, also in the cast); while on the stage she had to switch to the other end of the social scale and play a lesbian car mechanic with dreadlocks in the Bush Theatre's production of *The Chinese Wolf!*

The change was total once again when she was offered the part of Gemma Marshall.

'I was attracted by the strength and sparkiness of her character,' recalls Maureen. 'What was exciting about playing a woman in what is essentially a man's series was the fact that Gemma's a very sassy, powerful and intelligent character in her own right.

'There was also this twinkle in the eye between her and the Chief, which is another lovely side to play. Martin Shaw is an actor I have admired for a very long time – he is also extremely attractive – so it was very nice to twinkle away at someone who is nice to twinkle at!'

Of course, the pair clashed on their first encounter when Gemma was instrumental in getting a court room acquittal for Ian Dugeon, a man accused of murder by the Eastland police. Then, to rub salt into the wound, she persuaded her client to sue Cade for wrongful arrest.

There was never any question that Gemma was to be more than a match for the Chief. 'She was a maverick like him, you see. It was bound to be a fiery relationship with two people clashing all the time.'

Despite this, there was a mutual attraction between the pair. 'But Gemma's forthright views and her priority for justice had to come first. And if that meant putting at risk a relationship with the Chief and trampling over her own life, she would do it.'

Cade, for his part, was acutely aware that a police chief who associated with a radical lawyer in any kind of relationship would be under constant scrutiny by the Home Office, the media and the public.

Maureen says that Gemma was always driven by a sense of the injustice that exists in the world and was quite prepared to sacrifice her own emotional needs if necessary.

'There was never any way that she could be just another "new woman" for the Chief,' Maureen believes. 'If, as a woman, you are brought in to play a major part in someone's life there is always a tendency for you to end up lighting endless candles for endless dinners that you have prepared and which he can never be there to eat because he is too busy being a policeman, brain surgeon or pilot. The nice thing for me about Gemma was that she was just not that sort of person at all.'

The national newspaper reviewers were undoubtedly very taken by Maureen's 'fiery and powerful performance' (*Daily Telegraph*), with Andrew Preston of the *Daily Express* declaring emphatically that the courtroom battle between her and Cade, 'made sparks fly'.

Both Brenda Reid and Ruth Boswell would have liked Gemma Marshall to have continued in the fifth series.

'As a lawyer on the opposite side of the fence to the Chief there could have been excellent possibilities for tension in both their personal and professional lives,' says Ruth, who admits she had plans for the maverick lawyer to fall in love with Cade and become his lover.

'I was very keen on Gemma, too,' adds Brenda Reid regretfully. 'I think Maureen Beattie brought a lot to the character. But unfortunately she is not available to us. I suspect she will be missed by a lot of viewers.'

## THE GIRL FROM THE PAST
### Elena Belinsky (Louisa Haigh)

There have been few bigger surprises for Alan Cade since he took over as Chief Constable of Eastland than the sudden re-appearance in his life of his 21-year-old daughter, Elena. To a man who has grown used to not having a permanent relationship with a woman, this reminder of his most lasting affair causes a considerable upheaval to his emotions. Elena, who is now a post-graduate student at Cambridge University, is also strongly committed to a civil rights organization called Liberty Watch and as fiercely independent in her opinions about truth and justice as her father.

For the young, dark-haired actress Louisa Milwood Haigh the role provided her with the chance of playing opposite an actor she had admired for years – as well as helping to flesh out the Chief's family history.

'Until I appeared in the story, all Cade's relationships had been with women or professional people,' says Louisa. 'The producer thought it was time that he had someone to whom he could relate personally, but in a non-sexual way. Someone from his past with whom he could be very open and personal.'

Louisa's own past in the acting profession includes the role of Geraldine in the Nottingham Playhouse production of *What The Butler Saw* and appearances in a number of popular television series such as *Soldier, Soldier, The Men's Room, The Gemini Factor* and *Drop The Dead Donkey* where one of her co-stars was Ingrid Lacey. Her films have included leading roles in Brian Gibson's *Murderers Among Us (The Simon Weisenthall Story)*, *Shipwrecked* for Walt Disney Productions and Peter Greenaway's *The Baby of Maçon*. She came to *The Chief* from an appearance in that other highly-popular police drama series, *The Bill*.

The details of Alan Cade's life before he came to Eastland had only been briefly sketched in at this point of the series, although they did point to a checkered past. Elena, in fact, was from that part of his life before he even became a policeman: she was his child from a liaison during his student days in Paris. In 1968 while he was living in the city he had apparently met and fallen in love with another young student, a Canadian named Yvonne Belinsky. Both were full of the idealism of youth and later lived together for a time in London while Alan began to carve out his career in the Metropolitan Police. In 1973 Yvonne gave birth to Elena.

Cade undoubtedly loved his daughter, but his relationship with Yvonne began to fail as he rose up the ranks. Finally, Yvonne returned home to Toronto taking the baby with her.

'Though he wants to be a good father, Cade has always found it difficult to be involved with his daughter,' explains Louisa. 'He's only seen her about once every three or four years and so she hardly knows him at all. Part of the reason for this is that Yvonne has never really encouraged a strong rapport between them.'

The introduction of Elena also enabled an explanation to be given for Cade's radical views and attributes. Indeed, she herself was then taking a degree in International Law, specializing in Human Rights.

'Elena had been interested in politics ever since her childhood in Toronto,' says Louisa. 'In fact, she's been politically active from her teens and there was even a suggestion that she might have had a minor criminal record from an arrest during a student demonstration.'

At Cambridge, Elena's tutor was the radical lawyer, Gemma Marshall – who was also an adviser to Liberty Watch when not busy practising law. It was through Elena that Gemma first met Cade and thereby created an agonizing triangle of mixed emotions for the Chief as father, policeman and potential lover! For her part, Elena was instrumental in gaining justice for a Bosnian refugee who had died during a violent arrest.

Crucially, Elena's reunion with her father came at a time when he was at a nadir both emotionally and professionally. However, she was able to act as a moral catalyst forcing him to examine his own motivations and actions and even reflect on why he had joined the police in the first place. In one moving exchange she demanded of Cade: 'In the French riots in 1968 your girlfriend got injured by riot police and yet you still decided to be a policeman. I don't understand *why*.'

It was a dichotomy that Cade himself found difficult to answer, although as he listened to his daughter's passionate idealism he heard echoes of himself when young and was able to measure his own values against her youthful ideals of a just society.

'The story drew an interesting parallel with Cade's own student days,' says Louisa, 'and there is no doubt that Elena helped restore his fighting spirit. I think the result was an interesting father/daughter relationship which is always there if the series wanted to explore it further in the future . . . '

# 9

# THE MEN FROM THE MINISTRY

Series 1-5

## THE MACHIAVELLIAN UNDER SECRETARY
### Nigel Crimmond (Michael Cochrane)

Nigel Crimmond, the opportunist Deputy Permanent Under Secretary of State, has been a thorn in the side of both Chiefs. He is a man always quick to manipulate a politically sensitive situation to his own advantage and unforgiving of those who do not see eye to eye with his views.

As the man jointly responsible with the politician, Sir Anthony Maylor (Jeremy Clyde), for appointing John Stafford as Chief Constable, Crimmond was soon being made uncomfortably aware of the unpredictability of the person they had chosen. It's a situation that has not been improved with the arrival of Alan Cade, an even more radical Chief. The sparring between Crimmond and the two police officers has undoubtedly been one of the highlights of the series.

The twist of fate – or vageries of casting – which brought Michael Cochrane and Martin Shaw into the same series is not lost on Michael. For Cochrane is as passionately against flying as Martin Shaw is dedicated to it. Indeed, despite the fact that Michael became a household name as one of the Royal Air Force Flying Corps heroes in the BBC First World War series, *Wings*, he hates aeroplanes.

'I won't fly anywhere if I can help it,' he says. 'I'd much rather go by train or boat. I was very relieved at the time I was making *Wings* to learn I wouldn't have to fly. It was actually real pilots who did the aerobatic tricks and flying scenes. But it was a very good series.'

Playing the authoritative Crimmond with his smart suits and neatly brushed grey hair has, however, enabled Michael to keep his feet firmly on the ground and at the centre of Government as a high ranking civil servant who is responsible for police administration – including such things as intelligence interception, training, traffic, budgets and, most crucially, the running of police authorities. He is very much the mouthpiece of Government policy, an intelligent and articulate figure who moves effortlessly through the world of civil servants, ministers and politicians, while keeping his own counsel and manipulating his career, as well as those of others like the Chief.

The role is one to which Michael with his sparkling blue eyes and irrepressible sense of humour has brought considerable panache – though for some years he was rather better known in the newspapers as a lover of high jinks who had done little at school, lived a bohemian life in Paris for a while, and built up a reputation for enjoying a drink and chasing girls. He even had a real-life run-in with the forces of the law he came to so cleverly manouevre in *The Chief*.

'I got what I deserved,' he says with disarming honesty about the court case at Bow Street in January 1977 when he was fined for being drunk and disorderly. 'I had drinkies with a few chums and got a little bit upset with some chap who wouldn't stop honking his car horn. I found myself leapt on by some charming policemen and thrown into a cell for a couple of hours to cool off. But it was fair do's. I was quite rightly clobbered.'

Michael, known to his friends as 'Cockie', can smile now about this incident which earned him some mildly embarrassing headlines at the time he was shooting to stardom in *Wings*. In the series he played a dashing, upper-crust Hussars officer, Second Lieutenant Gaylion, a man who, in complete contrast to his own personality, saw flying as an extension of his priviliged life.

Cochrane the man is, though, undoubtedly something of an eccentric who now believes the acting profession is running short of personalities. His own eccentricities began as early as his schooldays in Newhaven, Sussex.

'I was a nincompoop at school, an absolute fool,' he reflects. 'A fair old fortune was spent on my education, but nothing came of it. I had this idea about being a writer or an actor. Then one day I was just driving through Brighton, stopped at the lights, saw this drama school, went in, and got interested.'

He also, he admits, got very interested in girls – and with his curly, golden hair and winning charm was never short of female company. His company director father, however, had other ideas and sent him off to Paris to study French. Here he preferred the existence of a bohemian on the Left Bank, earning his keep by writing and selling poetry to tourists. On several occasions, he says, he and a friend even jumped on to pleasure boats and faked stick-ups among the passengers to get free drinks. If they were challenged, they merely dived overboard and swam to the bank.

Nonetheless, Michael completed his course at the Brighton drama school before touring the provinces in rep to 'learn the trade'. The hard school of experience – on wages of £27 per week – gave him the expertise which has since enabled him to tackle a wide variety of roles, often as the educated types so different from his own upbringing. His credits include Lord Darlington in *Lady Windermere's Fan*, Darcy in *Pride and Prejudice*, Bassanio in *The Merchant Of Venice* at the Old Vic, and King George VI in a touring production of *Crown Matrimonial*.

On television Michael has been seen in several popular drama productions including Cedric in Thames TV's *Love In A Cold Climate*; as Freddie Hanson in BBC TV's *The Citadel*; and Sparkish in *The Country Wife* (BBC) directed by Donald McWhinnie with whom he has worked on a number of TV programmes. And apart from prominent roles in series such as *Warship*, *The Pallisters* and *Fortunes of War*, Michael has also appeared in John Huston's film, *Escape To Victory*, and *The Far Pavilions* directed by Peter Duffell. His previous experiences of crime on the box include London Weekend's series of *Agatha Christie Mysteries*, BBC's *The Detective* with Tom Bell, and *Rockliffe's Folly* which starred Ian Hogg.

Now in his mid-forties, Michael was delighted to accept the role of the suave, mustacheod Nigel Crimmond and has continued to play him right up to the fifth series when he is finally bowing out.

'The thing about Crimmond is that he has always been a manipulator,' says Michael, 'but when he finds that John Stafford is not the straight-down-the line police chief he had expected, and suddenly becomes this radical animal instead, he is in trouble for having been instrumental in appointing him. Stafford was forever causing him problems by going against the Establishment, the very thing he didn't want. I suppose you could call Nigel Crimmond the unacceptable face of government.'

Michael says that he has enjoyed his run-ins with both Chiefs – especially with Cade. 'Crimmond has the power to erode Cade's reputation and status by using innuendo and rumour. He does things like suggesting the Chief is politically naive or old fashioned in his views when he refuses to accept swinging changes in Government policies. He can even go as far as to suggest that in certain areas of policing Cade is not entirely to be trusted.'

Michael has developed the machiavellian streak in Crimmond very effectively during all five series, giving an added frisson to each appearance on screen. The Under Secretary's nomination of Cade for virtually hopeless assignments is also another example of the series drawing on real events – in this case the famous instance of John Stalker being sent to Northern Ireland and into a situation then impossible to resolve.

'It's all been great fun,' says Michael 'but all good things must come to an end. I have a film to make and it's time for Crimmond to bow out and make way for a new man from the Ministry. I hope he enjoys it as much as I have!'

# THE AGENT OF THE ESTABLISHMENT

## Colin Fowler (T P McKenna)

Former Chief Constable Colin Fowler has also been an adversary of both John Stafford and Alan Cade with his dedication to policing by the book and his habit of being a stickler for details. Whereas both of Eastland's Chiefs have been progressive thinkers, Fowler has always acted according to the maxim, 'knowledge is power' and constantly gathered information that he could put to use if and when the need arose. He has, in fact, used damaging information to undermine both men on a number of occasions.

As a member of the Inspectorate – the agents of the Home Secretary – Fowler is charged with keeping an eye on the operational effect of police chiefs. But although men like him are directly accountable to the Home Office, they have no executive power – but still wield considerable influence in the corridors of power.

The role of Fowler fitted the commanding figure of Irishman T P McKenna like the immaculate police uniform he invariably wore. Indeed, he quickly grabbed the attention of viewers in an early story when he confronted John Stafford in a heated television studio debate about the role of the police.

'Men like Fowler come from a kind of blueprint,' T P McKenna says in his gentle Irish burr. 'The members of the Inspectorate are all former Chief Constables – a bit like Stafford and Cade. But they are the ones who have listened to what they have been told by the Establishment. ''You be a good boy while you're Chief Constable and when you retire we'll give you a plum job''.

'Fowler was a man who had behaved himself well, so he was given this plum job. But there was no doubt about where his loyalty lay. He served his masters.'

McKenna, whose first names are Thomas Patrick and is usually called Tom by his friends, has been known by his initials ever since he began acting as a young man in Dublin. He is, though, in real life far from being the conformist he played in *The Chief*, having appeared in just about every kind of production from Shakespeare to cult TV programmes such as *Danger Man* and *The Avengers* during his forty years as a stage, film and television actor. He is a large, aimiable man who, in typical Irish fashion, often makes light of his many achievements.

He was born in Mullagh, County Cavan where the McKenna family have lived for almost 200 years. He was the eldest of ten children of a local auctioneer who nursed ambitions for him to become a successful businessman. The signs that this might not prove Tom's ultimate career were, however, evident early in his school days: he proved to be a 'star' boy soprano and was the hit of many performances at his boarding school.

'I think it is true to say I fell for the theatre when a touring company lead by Anew McMaster came through Mullagh,' he reflects. 'He and his players barnstormed our local town hall with their blood and lightning.'

Tom did, though, do as his father asked and worked in a bank in Dublin as a trainee manager. He completed five years in the job before the urge to go on the stage became too strong.

'I suppose I might still have been in the bank but for my inability to concentrate on studies for my examinations,' he continues. 'I was spending too much time doing amateur dramatics. So when they said they would send me back again to a country branch where there wouldn't be so many distractions, I quit and became an actor.'

Appropriately, it was the man he had watched in delight from the town hall auditorium who gave him his first chance.

'McMaster was the only actor in the world, you know, who could be marvellous in the first half of a line and terrible by the time he got to the end of it,' he says with a fond smile. 'Anyhow, I was 23, playing Horatio to his 63-year-old Hamlet. He did five shows, each got about a week of rehearsal and then straight on to the stage. ''Louder and faster'' was the only direction he ever gave us. A year later I joined the Abbey Theatre company and had to come down by about ten octaves. But I'd not have missed McMaster, not for all the world.'

In the following eight years, T P McKenna – as he was now billed – appeared in over 100 plays, all of them Irish. Although he felt this diet of local productions was 'like a sort of prison', it did earn him an enviable reputation in Ireland and he has since been made an Honorary Life Member of the company – one of only nine actors to be so honoured.

It was in February 1963 that McKenna finally broke away from Dublin and came to London to star in the St Martins Theatre production of *Steven D*, an adaptation of James Joyce's novel, *Portrait of the Artist as Young Man*. He followed this playing the part of O'Keefe in *The Ginger Man*, and ever since that his special brand of ebullience and sardonic humour has kept him in work in all three branches of the world of entertainment. In 1966 he won the award as Best Actor of the Year for his performance in *Who's Afraid of Virginia Woolf*.

Curiously, T P took on the role of Colin Fowler with a track record of only ever having played villains in crime stories before – which comes as something of a surprise to learn considering his benevolent appearance. He was, for instance, a hardened criminal in *The Strain* by the Welsh-Irish-Liverpool writer, Alun Owen. It

*The relationship between Fowler and Stafford was always volatile.*

was a play about gangs on Merseyside. He played the gang chief Fletcher in the Richard Burton movie, *Villain* and was also a murder victim in Brian Clements' story, 'Lady Killer' in the TV series, *Thriller*, in which he was unfortunately sent to his death by Robert Powell.

McKenna has, though, always been a little wary about what he calls the 'half-fame' accorded to actors by television and he explains why.

'On holiday, usually on a beach or at a bus stop, people will come up to you and say, "Are you on television?" "Yes," I say. "What do you do?" "I'm an actor." "But what series?" "I do plays, single plays." "No, no," they say, as if you're a bit slow, "but what series are you in?" I say, "I'm not in a series". Then they look at you in amazement and walk away. The sad fact is that in television unless you're in a series you might as well not exist.'

Despite these reservations about appearing on television – and the undeniable fact that T P McKenna has been a much appreciated actor with discerning audiences for years – he took the role of Fowler in *The Chief* without a second thought.

'Of course, I could just say I did it to pay the mortgage, as all actor's do,' he laughs, 'but actually I welcomed the chance to work on such a different kind of police series. Fowler was definitely a fascinating character, surprisingly narrow in his views despite a lifetime in the police force. He was a character very wary of change, I think, and especially worried by mavericks like Stafford and Cade.'

T P McKenna has, in fact, been very much a part of the success story of *The Chief* – but unfortunately, his character will not be re-appearing in the forthcoming fifth series.

He is now booked, instead, to return to his roots in Ireland and star in a new play in Dublin.

'After a while on television you feel the need to get back to the stage,' he explains. 'You have to get the muscles moving again, you have to feel an audience out there watching and listening. Otherwise you go dead.'

There is certainly no fear of T P McKenna dying in front of any audience whether in an auditorium or watching television in their living rooms. All the same, there is no doubt that many viewers of *The Chief* will miss the presence of the commanding 'Power Broker' Colin Fowler . . .

## A SMOOTH OPERATOR

### Andrew Blake (Julian Glover)

Andrew Blake, who has now replaced Colin Fowler as the Inspectorate's representative in Eastland in the fifth series, is a very sophisticated official used to operating at the highest levels of policing. He is, in fact, another former Chief Constable who has learned how to attain his objectives through a mixture of reason and subtle coercion, all applied with the practise born of years of experience.

'Blake is a man who knows which buttons to push,' says producer John Davies, 'how to get the people he is dealing with do what *he* wants.'

Julian Glover, who is playing Blake, is one of the country's foremost character actors, a man whose career on the stage, in films and on television has garnered him numerous awards. Only recently he won the Olivier award for his performance as Henry IV at Stratford and he remains one of the most in-demand performers around. Julian is also renowned as a splendid ensemble actor and he brings a strength of character and presence to his new role in *The Chief*.

Working on the series in East Anglia has also provided Julian with the chance to return to his roots, for he was actually brought up in the area in a tiny Essex village.

'One of my earliest memories is of walking across the village green for my first day at school,' he says. 'On the way, I bent down to do up the lace of one of my shoes and a boy who was playing nearby with some others came up and gave me a kick in the bottom. I fell flat on my face in the mud. But instead of crying I got up laughing and soon all the other boys were too. It seemed I had a talent to amuse!'

Julian has less painful memories of returning to East Anglia in 1985 when he co-starred with Roy Marsden in Anglia's adaptation of the P D James' crime novel, *Cover Her Face*.

'The director was John Davies,' Julian recalls, 'so it is nice to be associated with him again on *The Chief*. We spent a lot of time filming scenes in some of the loveliest parts of Norfolk and I'm looking forward to doing so again.'

It is quite evident that Andrew Blake is a rather different character to Colin Fowler. Where Fowler would confront Cade, he is more inclined to take him into his confidence.

'I'm here to help, not interfere, Alan,' he announces to Cade at their first introduction in episode one. 'If there is anything I can do – pull strings – let me know.'

Blake's own experiences in the police force have helped him to understand a liberal like Cade. Prior to his appointment to the Inspectorate he was the Chief Constable of Avon and Somerset after a distinguished career in which he had served in several areas not unlike Eastland and which also had faced the same kind of problems. Indeed, he is to be reminded of his past in the series when his former deputy, Brian Webster – who has now assumed his role as the Chief – becomes involved in accusations of spying on his number two.

Julian's own personal history is one of dedication to his profession which has been rewarded with a series of interesting roles. He was born the son of C Gordon Glover, a journalist and broadcaster, and Honor Wyatt, a novelist and producer of *Woman's Hour*. After a few years in Essex, Julian moved with his mother to Bristol where they spent the years of the Second World War. During this time he had a narrow escape from danger when he was out playing near the Clifton Gorge and innocently walked into a hut which proved to be full of live ammunition!

Julian did not originally envisage a career in acting. 'I assumed I'd be a journalist like my parents, but though I'm persistent and stubborn I lacked their grit and drive. I was only good at English.'

In fact, it was a visit to Sadlers Wells with his mother that opened his eyes to the world of drama and she has, he says, been his greatest source of encouragement ever since. In a recent interview, Honor Wyatt explained of her son: 'He has a ruthless streak, despite his warmth and kindness and a heart as large as the Atlantic.'

Julian attended Alleyn's School in West Dulwich where he first went on the stage as Anthony in *Julius Caesar*. One of his tutors at the school was Michael Croft who later founded Britain's National Youth Theatre which fostered the talents of several now-famous thespians including Simon Ward, Helen Mirren and Julian himself.

Now, sure in his own mind what he wanted his career to be, he studied at RADA and then worked for several repertory companies at Bromley, Wimbledon and Brighton before joining the Royal Shakespeare Company where he cut his teeth on most of the great classical roles. While with the RSC he went on their prestigious tour of Russia.

Julian made his film debut playing a villainous lieutenant in Tony Richardson's version of the bawdy eighteenth century romp, *Tom Jones*, and has since, he says, 'played a lot more villains in countless Wednesday plays, on Saturday Night Theatre and in a large number of TV series.'

He received fine reviews for his performance in another Tony Richardson movie, *Dead Cert*, based on a Dick Francis novel, in which he played a corrupt policeman, Inspector Lodge, in the pay of a racecourse doping gang known as Whiteleys who ran a protection racket as well as 'fixing' races. However, not every role offered to him has been to play a 'baddie', as he is very quick to point out.

'I was once up for the part of James Bond when Sean Connery dropped out,' he says, 'and I came pretty close to getting it. The ironic thing is they did later cast me in *For Your Eyes Only* when Roger Moore was Bond. I played Kristatos and the audience were kept guessing all the time as to whether I or Columbo, played by Topol, was the villain!'

His intimate knowledge of the other side of the law has enabled Julian to bring a special edge to his performance as Andrew Blake. His fascination with the use of words which he inherited from his mother has also given him an ability to deliver telling lines with quite startling impact.

Working in East Anglia allows Julian to get home to West London to his actress wife, Isla Blair, and their son, Jamie, without much difficulty when he is not required for filming. Jamie has already had a taste of the theatrical life his parents follow when he appeared with his father at the tender age of eight in *Coriolanus* at Stratford.

In *The Chief*, Julian is enjoying working with both Martin Shaw and Michael Cochrane whom he has known for some years. His exchanges with Cochrane playing Nigel Crimmond promise some of the best moments in the new series.

It is as a result of Blake's recommendation that the Home Office has approved Wes Morton as Cade's number two, and the inspector is ready to defend his Eastland people against Crimmond's barbed remarks.

'We are working on the same side,' he tells the Under Secretary in episode one, only for Crimmond to respond in typical fashion: 'What a wonderful world *that* would be.'

Blake is a man who believes that a tough line needs to be taken with young offenders to prevent them turning into hardened criminals, and is quick to warn Cade not to let his heart rule his head in emotive situations.

The relationship between Andrew Blake and Alan Cade is one of the key elements in the fifth series as it builds towards a climax. Indeed, it is Blake who makes one of the most tantalizing remarks about the future of the Chief in episode three when solicitously enquiring if Cade plans to spend the rest of his career in Eastland.

'And where would I want to go from here?' Cade says.

'There's always the top job at the Met,' Blake answers with an enigmatic smile, 'when it comes up next . . .'

# 10

# THE CHIEF

Episode Guide and Credits

## SERIES 1

**Episode One by Jeffrey Caine**
As the series opens Stafford is hurled in at the deep end with a crisis looming at a local prison with the prison officers in dispute. Stafford is under pressure from the Home Office to send in his men to prevent a riot but he challenges the ruling, and deals with the problem in his own indomitable fashion.

Assistant Chief Constable Anne Stewart is concerned for the welfare of a female remand prisoner who refuses to eat. Anne's fears prove correct as the prisoner commits suicide before the doctor is able to help.

Stafford also faces problems on the home front when his rebellious son Tim gets involved in a protest demonstration against a new marina development.

**Episode Two by Jeffrey Caine**
Stafford's order to destroy Special Branch files on so-called subversives angers local Tory MP Sir Ian Harnett. Over a game of golf with the Head of Special Branch the politician plots to ensure the files fall into the hands of MI5 before they reach the shredder. There's more trouble for Stafford with his rebellious son Tim again, when he is arrested while on a joy ride with friends and is accused of possessing cannabis.

**Episode Three by Jeffrey Caine**
Anne Stewart is determined to quash vicious allegations, made by Chief Supt McKay, against the Chief Constable, that Stafford ordered no action to be taken against his son when he was arrested for possessing cannabis. Anne suspects that the arresting officer planted the drug on Tim Stafford, a theory which later proves correct.

Meanwhile the controversial Special Branch files which Stafford ordered to be shredded have been passed to MI5 and Tory MP Sir Ian Harnett finds himself at the centre of a political scandal.

**Episode Four by Jeffrey Caine**
Terry Slater and his mate Winston Daniels believe the police are doing nothing to crack down on the drug dealers on their estate and plot a raid on a pub. But John Stafford decides to make a personal visit to the vigilantes to promise better policing.

The Chief's interference with MI5 and Special Branch files is landing him in hot water at the Home Office. Sir Alan Stourby, the Inspector of Constabulary, warns Stafford that his position is in jeopardy.

**Episode Five by Jeffrey Caine**
Chief Inspector Hedger woos a young policewoman while indulging in dirty tricks to descredit his boss, Chief Constable Stafford. While he is gathering damning evidence against the Chief, a drugs raid on a pub develops into a violent affray, and an innocent bystander is injured.

Emma Stafford warns her father of trouble brewing among her fellow students, who are planning a protest against a visiting Government minister. Det Chief Supt Jim Gray warns businessman, and fellow mason, Howard Reeves that he is under investigation for fraud.

### Episode Six by Jeffrey Caine

Investigative journalist Martin Scobie uncovers a Masonic plot to discredit Stafford. He informs Anne Stewart of his investigations which reveal damning evidence being gathered against Stafford.

Meanwhile Stafford clashes with the authorities when he refuses to forcibly evict protesting university students who are occupying a building. He is summoned to the Home Office for a meeting with Sir Anthony Maylor, jeopardising his future.

### Cast List

| | |
|---|---|
| Chief Constable | |
| John Stafford | TIM PIGOTT SMITH |
| Assistant Chief Constable | |
| Anne Stewart | KAREN ARCHER |
| Dr Elizabeth Stafford | JUDY LOE |
| Major Selwyn Davis | FREDERICK JAEGER |
| Detective Chief Superintendent | |
| Jim Gray | EAMON BOLAND |
| Sir Ian Harnett | JULIAN HOLLOWAY |
| Nigel Crimmond | MICHAEL COCHRANE |
| Detective Chief Inspector | |
| George Hedger | TREVOR BYFIELD |
| Terence Ogilvy | JOHN WOODVINE |
| Charlie Summers | DAVID RYALL |
| Howard Reeves | KEN FARRINGTON |
| Martin Scobie | DUDLEY SUTTON |
| Detective Superintendent | |
| Brian Kale | STEPHEN TATE |
| Sir Anthony Maylor | JEREMY CLYDE |
| Martin Stewart | DAVID CARDY |
| Emma Stafford | SARA GRIFFITHS |
| Tim Stafford | ROSS LIVINGSTONE |
| Norman Ames | TERENCE HARVEY |
| Sir Alan Stourby | WILFRED HARRISON |

### Crew List

| | |
|---|---|
| Producer | RUTH BOSWELL |
| Director | BRIAN FARNHAM |
| Executive Producer | BRENDA REID |
| Designer | DON HOMFRAY |
| Music | NIGEL BEAHAM-POWELL |
| | BELLA RUSSELL |
| Casting | PAT JARVIS |
| Lighting | ROGER LAW |
| | KEVIN WINCH |
| VT Editor | ALAN NEWTON |
| Police Adviser | JOHN ALDERSON |

## SERIES 2

*A dramatic stunt from the second series filmed on location in Norwich.*

### Episode One by Jeffrey Caine

Stafford returns after his suspension to find ACC Quine dealing with a series of hoax bomb calls from animal rights group Biteback. This is in fact a lone operator, Ian Williams. He plants a fake bomb in a department store, then warns of one in a lab. So when a warning comes of another bomb hidden in a consignment of mink at Felixstowe, the bomb squad do not take it very seriously. The blast kills two Eastland officers. Stafford has to take responsibility for his officers' negligence.

Anne arrests Williams; meanwhile the real culprit, a French animal activist, escapes to the continent.

**Episode Two by Jeffrey Caine**

Stafford and Fowler have an aggressive confrontation on TV about modern policing.

Meanwhile a series of break-ins on an up-market estate leads to calls for private security. A schizophrenic named Rudyard abducts a 14-year-old runaway and holds him captive at the mental home where he was a former patient. The break-ins are found to be the work of private security guards.

**Episode Three by Jeffrey Caine**

Martin Stewart leaves his wife Anne. A DI is accused of sexually assaulting his young WDC. Anne champions her case. Anne tries for a reconciliation with her husband, but is rejected.

Meanwhile the siege at the mental hospital grows more tense and the boy's life is endangered. Stafford orders the marksman to kill Rudyard.

**Episode Four by Jeffrey Caine**

An investigative journalist makes a programme about the spread of BSE, 'mad cow disease' from animals to humans, based on a leaked government document. The Home Office is alerted and orders its seizure by Deputy Quine. Stafford, who has been away, is furious at his misapplication of the law.

He warns Keenan of the impending injunction and the programme is transmitted, causing an uproar. Crimmond upbraids Stafford for being irresponsible.

**Episode Five by Jeffrey Caine & Peter Palliser**

A murder investigation is set up on a rough estate after two boys throw a brick at a police officer, killing him. Stafford confronts the people of the estate and tries to negotiate with them: better policing in exchange for information about the killers.

**Episode Six by Jeffrey Caine & Peter Palliser**

A child playing on a beach gets poisoned with dioxin containing tar, the result of a tanker spillage. Meanwhile, protesters from environmental group Globewatch demonstrate against a ship with a cargo of mercury waste bound for South Africa.

Crimmond orders Stafford to evict them for trespassing when they board the ship. Stafford refuses. He is offered the Europol job by the Home Office, 'kicked upstairs' as he sees it, and encourages Anne to aim for his job.

---

## Cast List

| | |
|---|---|
| Chief Constable | |
| John Stafford | TIM PIGOTT SMITH |
| Assistant Chief Constable | |
| Anne Stewart | KAREN ARCHER |
| Dr Elizabeth Stafford | JUDY LOE |
| Colin Fowler | T P McKENNA |
| Kenneth Rudyard | ROGER LLOYD PACK |
| DCS Arthur Quine | TONY CAUNTER |
| Billie Keenan | KIKA MARKHAM |
| Nigel Crimmond | MICHAEL COCHRANE |
| DCS Jim Gray | EAMON BOLAND |
| DS Powers | SEAN PERTWEE |
| Martin Stewart | DAVID CARDY |
| Sir Anthony Maylor | JEREMY CLYDE |
| Sir Alan Stourby | WILFRED HARRISON |
| Tim Stafford | ROSS LIVINGSTONE |
| Emma Stafford | SARA GRIFFITHS |
| Councillor Alec Radcliffe | GARY WALDHORN |
| Councillor Mrs Morpeth | ROWENA COOPER |
| Dr Hajib | RENU SETNA |
| Diane Lewis | GILLIAN MARTELL |
| DS Tony Pelham | SIMON SLATER |
| Pattie Coldwell | PATTIE COLDWELL |

---

## Crew List

| | |
|---|---|
| Producer | RUTH BOSWELL |
| Director | DESMOND DAVIS |
| Executive Producer | BRENDA REID |
| Designer | JON PUSEY |
| Music | NIGEL BEAHAM-POWELL |

Casting . . . . . . . . . . . . .ROGER DAVIDSON
Associate Producer . . . . . . . .KIT WILLIAMS
Lighting . . . . . . . . . .MALCOLM HARRISON
                           KEVIN WINCH
VT Editor . . . . . . . . . . .RICHARD KENNAN
Costume . . . . . . . . . . . . .PRUE HANDLEY
Make-Up . . . . . . . . . . . .JANE ATKINSON
                        LOUISE WILLSHER

## Production

Coordinator . . . . . . .SUZANNE DUNCANSON
Continuity . . . . . . . . .CHRISTINE WILSON
Unit Production Manager . . .TREVOR VAISEY
1st Assistant Director . . . . . .BILL BRENNAN
2nd Assistant Director . . . .AVERIL BRENNAN
3rd Assistant Director . . .STEPHEN SENDALL
Production Buyer . . . . . . . . .POLLY BURNS
Cameras . . . . . . . . . . . .JULES GREENWAY
                          PAUL BALDWIN
Police Adviser . . . . . . . . .JOHN ALDERSON

## SERIES 3

### Episode One by Peter Jukes
John Stafford has accepted his invitation
from Brussels to become Head of Europol.
But in the meantime he has time to spare
and the Home Office ask him to head an
enquiry into corruption in the Metropolitan
Police Force.

As both acting Chief and Deputy of
Eastland, ACC Anne Stewart heads the
search for a Territorial Army private who
has gone AWOL shooting and killing a
policeman. Her decision to supervise the
incident personally costs her the
appointment to the Deputyship.

### Episode Two by Peter Jukes
In London, Stafford is approached by
Deputy Assistant Commissioner Alan Cade
who is prepared to aid the corruption
enquiry. With his help the enquiry is
successfully concluded. Cade goes on to
impress the Eastland selection committee,
who appoint him as their new Chief
Constable.

### Episode Three by Ray Jenkins
Cade's first day is every Chief Constable's
worst nightmare as a massive American gas
rig is hijacked off the Norfolk coast. The
hijackers, three ex-oil riggers, demand
better safety standards throughout the
industry. Despite the Home Office putting
pressure on Cade, he refuses to use force.
Instead he allows Anne Stewart to be flown
on to the rig and her success at negotiating
with the hijackers confirms Cade's faith in
her as his Acting Deputy and Head of CID.

### Episode Four by Ray Jenkins
A hospital laboratory technician implicates
a local Councillor in illegal working
practices and when he fears the police are
not acting on his information he breaks
through the security cordons during a Royal
visit to a local school concert to the
embarrassment of the new Chief Constable.

### Episode Five by Ray Jenkins
A brutally disfigured body is found in a
quarry and the murder enquiry uncovers a
trail leading to a large-scale drug smuggling
operation. In the pursuit of the drug
baron Cade allows the use of a police
informant as a mole to complete a drugs
pick-up by boat, which leads him to his
death. This decision exposes Cade to heavy
criticism.

### Episode Six by Ray Jenkins
In Newmarket a young DC is critically
injured by a group of bank robbers who
then disappear into the crowds of daily
racegoers. The odds are stacked against the
emotionally charged team of detectives who
desperately search for the assailants.

Mrs Maxwell, Chairperson of the Police
Authority, is stunned to discover that her
husband has been cautioned for soliciting
prostitutes. Cade's policy of giving two
cautions before an arrest is seen by some
as currying favour with the authorities.

However, his loyal team of senior officers stand by him when he is threatened with investigation over the death of the drugs informer. But Cade is not given the chance publicly to exonerate himself, as the Home Office believe they will wield more power over him if he feels he is in their debt. They do not know the true Alan Cade . . .

## Cast List

Chief Constable
John Stafford . . . . . . . . .TIM PIGOTT SMITH
Deputy Assist. Commissioner
Alan Cade . . . . . . . . . . . . .MARTIN SHAW
Assistant Chief Constable
Anne Stewart . . . . . . . . . .KAREN ARCHER
Marie-Pierre Arnoux . . . . . .JULIETTE MOLE
Dr Elizabeth Stafford . . . . . . . . . .JUDY LOE
Nigel Crimmond . . . .MICHAEL COCHRANE
Colin Fowler . . . . . . . . . . . .T P McKENNA
Sir Anthony Maylor . . . . . .JEREMY CLYDE
David Kendal . . . . . . . . . . . .DAVID HUNT
Cllr Rosaline Maxwell . . . . . .KATE BINCHY
Edgar Maxwell . . . . . . . . .ROBERT SWANN
Cllr Samuel Winstanley . . . . . .JOHN CATER
Cllr Mani Shankar . . . . . .AYUB KHAN-DIN
Cllr Jack Welford . . . . . . . .SHAUN CURRY
Det. Chief Supt Jim Gray . . .EAMON BOLAND
De. Supt Sean McCloud . .STUART McGUGAN
Andy Stewart . . . . . . . . .WILLIAM TURNER
Ben Stewart . . . . . . . . . . . .PAUL LEONARD
Diane Lewis . . . . . . . . .GILLIAN MARTELL
PC Jack Sayers . . . . . . . . . .DEAN LEPLEY

## Crew List

Executive Producer . . . . . . . .BRENDA REID
Director . . . . . . . . . . . . . . . . . .A J QUINN
Producer . . . . . . . . . . . . .RUTH BOSWELL
Executive in charge
of Production . . . . . . .DAVID FITZGERALD
Production Designer . . . . .JONATHAN PUSEY
Associate Producer . . . . . . . .KIT WILLIAMS
Music . . . . . . . . .NIGEL BEAHAM-POWELL
BELLA RUSSELL
Editor . . . . . . . . . . . . . . . . .KEITH JUDGE

Cameras . . . . . . . . . . . . .PETER EVESON
PAUL BALDWIN
Lighting . . . . . . . . . . . . . .CHRIS BROWN
PHILIP BURNE
Casting . . . . . . . . . . . . . .SUSIE BRUFFIN
Script Editor . . . . . . . . . . .ROSY WILLIAMS
Make-up . . . . . . . . . . . . . . .PENNY HUNT
Costume . . . . . . . . . . . . . .PRUE HANDLEY
Art Director . . . . . . . . . .KIRSTEN DUDLEY
Production Buyer . . . . . . . . .GILL DUCKER
POLLY BURNS
Sound . . . . . . . . . . . . . . .MIKE PINCHIN
Dubbing Mixers . . . . . . . .COLIN GILCHRIST
BILL PICTON
Technical Co-ordinator . . . . .SPIKE THORNE
1st Assistant Director . . . . .GERRY WIGZELL
2nd Assistant Director . . . . . . . . .TOM HUNT
Unit Production Manager . . . .TED WILLIAMS
Production Co-ordinator . . . . . . .SUE HEARD
Continuity . . . . . . . . . .CHRISTINE WILSON
Locations . . . . . . . .ANDREW RAWLINSON
NICK DUVALL
Special Effects . . . . . . . . . .ARTHUR BEVIS
Police Adviser . . . . . . . . .JOHN ALDERSON

## SERIES 4

**Episode One by Peter Jukes**
Chief Constable Alan Cade is at the centre of public outrage after two terrorist bomb-blasts in Eastland. The first – planted in a litter bin – injures shoppers in the busy Haywain Centre. The second – on a train taking cubs on the seaside holiday – kills a woman and injures five children. Cade clashes with the anti-terrorist squad over their tactics for flushing out the IRA unit responsible. Their interference puts his reputation on the line.

Cade is gradually drifting away from his French girlfriend, Marie-Pierre, and when she realizes that his long-term commitment to Eastland is deeper than at first either of them had suspected, she finally makes the break and takes up the offer of a job abroad.

**Episode Two by Ray Jenkins**
A party of illegal Chinese immigrants arrives in Eastland in a secret operation to ferry Hong Kong nationals from Belgium to England. But one of the party is recognized as a Triad, and is attacked by an organizer waiting to take the party to their new homes. The Triad dies in a ball of flames on the airport runway, and his death triggers a campaign of terror by Triad gangs, eager to hunt down the illegal immigrants. Chief Constable Cade is determined to halt the revenge attacks, and to uncover who is responsible for the illegal immigrants.

On a political level, Cade tracks down the crooked Belgian diplomat responsible for supplying the Orientals with their forged passports.

**Episode Three by Ray Jenkins**
Acting Deputy Chief Constable Anne Stewart is disillusioned and frustrated when she still doesn't win the promotion she has been fighting for. Inspector of Constabulary Colin Fowler, and Chief Inspector of Constabulary Sir David Leeson, make her an offer she can't refuse. With proposed changes in the police force, they want to strengthen the inspectorate, and they think Anne is the woman to help them.

Meanwhile a young mum – Stephanie – becomes a police informer to help catch youths who broke into a flat and beat up an old lady. But Stephanie becomes the victim of revenge attacks.

**Episode Four by Michael Russell**
Pushy public relations executive Alison Dell has a few candid comments for Chief Constable Cade about sharpening up his image. She tells him a public opinion poll in Eastland showed he was unpopular and his leadership was not re-assuring. Displeased by her comments, but impressed by her diligence, Cade agrees to employ Alison to boost the force's image. And their working relationship spills over into their private lives.

Meanwhile, an undercover operation by a team of customs and excise officers goes disastrously wrong, leaving a young constable seriously injured.

**Episode Five by Michael Russell**
Pregnant Hilary Scott is met by a barrage of abuse from anti-abortion protesters as she arrives at an Eastland clinic. Scared by the vociferous campaign and the terrifying tactics of the protesters, Hilary goes home to think about the abortion. Meanwhile the protesters' campaign is reinforced with the arrival from America of leading anti-abortionist Dan Cheyney. Cheyney uses a service at the cathedral as the platform for his campaign, where Chief Constable Cade and Alison Dell are among the congregation.

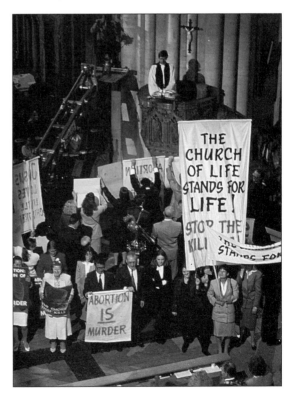

*Anti-abortion demonstrators amass in a cathedral during the fourth series.*

As the Dean delivers a sermon about abortion, supporting the right for women to choose, Cheyney and his evangelical supporters hoist placards and hurl verbal abuse at the pulpit.

### Episode Six by Michael Russell

Eastland Drugs Squad carry out a surveillance operation followed by a swift raid, arresting the leading drug pushers in the area. But the Community Liaison Officer recognizes the need for a more long-term solution and feels that as a police officer he cannot offer one.

A more dubious solution is offered when it is discovered that Cade's unit in the Drugs Squad at the Met is under investigation for fitting up suspected villains.

Cade is questioned about his role during his time at the Yard. Cade is clean, but his ex-DCS admits that he could see it as the only way to catch the chief drug traffickers.

### Episode Seven by Peter Jukes

Security is at a premium when Cade invites one of Italy's top anti-Mafia judges, Pietro Donati, to address a Europol conference on the world's fight against drugs. The conference coincides with the introduction of his own controversial initiative to tackle the drug problem in Eastland. During an unscheduled visit to Cade's house, Donati is shot and wounded by one of his bodyguards. Recognizing much of himself in Donati, Cade vows to continue his campaign against drugs.

DC Corbyn is investigating steroid abuse and its link with violent behaviour. He suspects Ian Dudgeon of dealing in steroids. Dudgeon's girlfriend Lisa packs to leave him because of his violence. He tries to wrench the carrycot containing their baby daughter from Lisa, and it smashes against a wall, killing the child.

### Episode Eight by Peter Jukes

Defence Barrister Gemma Marshall takes up Ian Dudgeon's case – he is in court accused of murdering his daughter. In intense cross examination of the prosecution's main witness – a deaf old lady who lives next door to the couple – Gemma throws doubt on her evidence. Dudgeon is freed and vows to sue the Chief Constable for wrongful arrest and false imprisonment. Chief Constable Cade is being tailed by a mystery woman. She emerges as his daughter Elena who he hasn't seen for five years – a shock for colleagues who know nothing of his past.

### Episode Nine by Brian Smith

A gang from a neo-Nazi group, Blood and Homeland, plans to raid the home of Councillor Mani Shankar. Murray, a police officer working undercover as a member of the gang, leaks the information to Special Branch. As the gang approaches the house, leader Dean Clark spots a police sniper. He sets out to punish the person who has grassed on them.

A Blood and Homeland rally ends in chaos when anti-Nazi protesters turn up. But Cade insists they have as much right to be at the public meeting as the Blood and Homeland supporters.

### Episode Ten by Michael Russell

Immigration officers working with Eastland Police and a private security firm swoop on immigrants working on farmland without visas. But the force used to restrain one worker as he struggles to resist arrest leads to his death. Chief Constable Cade calls in a team from West Mercia Police to investigate the circumstances. Simon Duval, head of the security firm, sacks all his men involved in the tragedy.

Gemma Marshall as the representative of the civil liberties group Liberty Watch calls for a public inquiry to discover why these

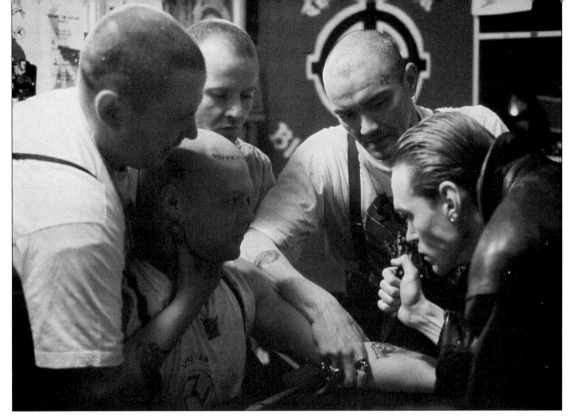

*Members of the neo-Nazi group, Blood and Homeland, prove a threat to law and order in series 4*

people were being used as slave labour. Cade learns that he is on the shortlist to head a new national CID, and Duval makes a job offer to Anne Stewart.

## Cast List

Chief Constable Alan Cade . . .MARTIN SHAW
Assistant Chief Constable
Anne Stewart . . . . . . . . . .KAREN ARCHER
Ch. Supt Sean McCloud . .STUART McGUGAN
David Kendal . . . . . . . . . . .SIMON SLATER
Nigel Crimmond . . . . .MICHAEL COCHRANE
Colin Fowler . . . . . . . . . . . . .T P McKENNA
Alison Dell . . . . . . . . . . . . .INGRID LACEY
Gemma Marshall . . . . .MAUREEN BEATTIE
Hilary Scott . . . . . . . . .CATHERINE CUSACK
Marie-Pierre Arnoux . . . . . .JULIETTE MOLE
Diane Lewis . . . . . . . . .GILLIAN MARTELL
Jack Sayers . . . . . . . . . . . . .DEAN LEPLEY
Mani Shankar . . . . . . . . . .AYUB KHAN DIN
Elena Belinsky . . . . . . . . . .LOUISA HAIGH
Simon Duval . . . . . . . . . . . . .PETER EGAN
Donati . . . . . . . . . . . . . . . .BRUCE MYERS
DC Corbyn . . . . . . . . . . . .JOHN McARDLE

## Crew List

Executive Producer . . . . . . . .BRENDA REID
Directors . . . . . . . . . . . . . . . .A J QUINN
ROGER GARTLAND
Producer . . . . . . . . . . . . .RUTH BOSWELL
Executive in charge
of production . . . . . . . .DAVID FITZGERALD
Production Designers . . . .JONATHAN PUSEY
SPENCER CHAPMAN
Associate Producers . . . . . . . .KIT WILLIAMS
ELIZABETH HARE
Music . . . . . . . . .NIGEL BEAHAM-POWELL
BELLA RUSSELL
Editors . . . . . . . . . . . . . . . .KEITH JUDGE
ALAN NEWTON
Directors of Photography . . . . . .ROGER LAW
PHILIP BURNE
Camera Operator . . . . . . . . .PETER EVESON
Casting . . . . . . . . . . . . . . . .SARAH BIRD
CELIA PEART
Script Editors . . . . . . . . . .ROSY WILLIAMS
LOUISE RANCE
Make-up . . . . . . . . . . . . . . .PENNY HUNT
LOUISE WILLSHER

*Cade, with the beautiful South American exile, Maria Romero (Shelagh McLeod) in the latest series.*

| | |
|---|---|
| Costume | REG SAMUEL |
| Art Director | KIRSTEN DUDLEY |
| Production Buyers | POLLY BURNS |
| | BILL FAWCETT |
| Sound | MIKE PINCHIN |
| Dubbing Mixers | RICHARD COLLINS |
| | COLIN GILCHRIST |
| 1st Assist. Directors | GERRY WIGZELL |
| | BILL BRENNAN |
| 2nd Assist. Directors | LEAF WIGZELL |
| | TOM HUNT |
| 3rd Assist. Director | PETER CURZON |
| Unit Production Managers | TED WILLIAMS |
| | TREVOR VAISEY |
| Production Co-ordinator | SUE HEARD |
| Continuity | CHRISTINE WILSON |
| | SALLY MONTAGUE |
| Locations | ANDREW RAWLINSON |
| Special Effects | ARTHUR BEAVIS |
| | DEREK LANGLEY |
| Stunt Arranger | ALAN STUART |
| Police Adviser | JOHN ALDERSON |

## SERIES 5

**Episode One: 'One Of Our Own' by Maggie Allen from a story by Reg Gadney**

Alan Cade is returning home from a firearms training session which he has undertaken reluctantly when he intercepts a message about a break-in at Brackley Grange. The Chief attempts to put his training into effect and detain the three armed and masked robbers but his driver is shot in the hail of gunfire. In another part of Eastland, the home of the Van Mullem family is being watched as part of an undercover operation by the Regional Crime Squad officers investigating an illegal arms deal.

The fatal wounding of the driver makes Cade and his men pull out all the stops to catch the three villains, while at the same time the net closes tighter around the latest shipment of arms about to enter the country from Holland. A journalist investigating the illegal arms story very nearly jeopardizes the entire operation just as the police are about to storm the Van Mullen farmhouse.

**Episode Two: 'Something To Lose' by Len Collin**

Maria Romero, whose husband was a Chief of Police in Paranagua until his car was bombed by agents of the new regime, seeks political asylum in a church in Eastland. When Alan Cade refuses to arrest her on charges of drug smuggling, rumours abound that she is a former girlfriend. A new police initiative to help persistent offenders by offering them driving lessons is also under threat, and matters come to a head when a car, which has been stolen by joy-riders, knocks down and kills a young cyclist. Cade is once again accused of being soft on crime.

The Home Office is concerned about the Chief's failure to act on the situation regarding Maria Romero, and the immigration authorities step in and arrest her. Cade's strong beliefs see him in confrontation with the law over Maria, and then with a section of the public who want to take the law into their own hands over the death of the cyclist.

### Episode Three: 'Old Scores' by Anthony Read

A by-election in Eastland is disrupted when the skinhead supporters of an ultra-right-wing candidate of the Patriotic Party are involved in a skirmish with a group of Pakistani youths which ends with one of the Asians left dying. Two police officers who were acting as observers and then intervened in the fight are subsequently accused by both the candidate and the head of the Asian community as having been instrumental in the death. The Chief at once orders a full enquiry to be held.

Suspicions also start to grow about the past activities of the Chairman of the Eastland Police Authority who had lived in Africa for many years, when a young woman researching a book about the independence struggle of Zimbabwe mentions his name to Cade in connection with a brutal slaying. The Chief faces a similar quandary about just what kind people he is dealing with when the evidence begins to mount up against his two officers and the fact that one is concealing far more than he admits about what really occurred after the election meeting.

### Episode Four: 'Taking Liberties' by Steve Griffiths

A major demonstration is taking place against the Hopefield Nuclear Power Station on the coast of Eastland. It is led by a young mother whose son died of leukaemia, which she believes was caused by the plant. When Cade is asked to stop the disruption to the work of the station by the manager, he listens to both sides and says that he also has a duty to protect freedom of speech.

While the argument continues to rage,

Cade is called away to investigate allegations against a senior officer in the Mid-Pennine Police Force who is accused of having an affair with the wife of a well-known local criminal. In his absence, a group of trouble makers known as the Eco-Warriors arrive at Hopefield and turn the formerly peaceful protest to violence by firing steel balls from catapaults and setting off smoke cannisters. As Cade brings his investigation into the charges against the Mid-Pennine officer to a conclusion, he learns of the disturbance back at the nuclear plant and is furious that his men have allowed the incident to escalate.

*The Eastland officers were forced to don protective clothing when arresting protestors against a Nuclear Power Station in series five.*

### Episode Five: 'Pressure' by Ian Kennedy Martin

A CID officer is involved in an accident with a young motorcyclist while speeding to the scene of the Eastland Police's aborted mission to watch over a meeting of suspected drug dealers. Two detectives arrive to keep surveillance on a Detective Inspector Jack Bertrand, recently retired from Chelsea CID who has taken a cottage in Eastland. He is suspected of involvement in a conspiracy to conceal the proceeds of a robbery. The Chief's emotions are torn, particularly as Bertrand once saved his life during a stakeout at a bank, that went horribly wrong.

### Episode Six: 'Drawing the Line' by Susan Wilkins

Tom Breseter, a County Councillor and member of the Eastland Police Authority is outraged when his son confesses to being homosexual, and is associated with the new owner of Ransley Hall, Archie Camfield. One of his notorious parties is raided by the police but there are also darker suggestions that Camfield is laundering money through his art dealing business. Cade tries to mediate between Brewster and his son, and finds himself being drawn closer to Maria Romero. One of DS Rose Penfold's female colleagues lodges a complaint against a male colleague, of sexual harassment.

### Episode Seven by Ian Kennedy Martin

The body of the wife of local farmer John Halkin, is found in the Fens and there are signs that she has been murdered. DC Rose Penfold takes charge, as the Chief is on holiday. The following day, under the headline, 'The Maverick Chief' the *Chronicle* makes a number of serious allegations against Cade. The Chief opts to remain on holiday with Sir Richard Gooding, hoping to decide whether he wants to remain Chief. Rose reaches crisis point in her relationship with her husband. For both, the future is very much in the balance . . .

## Cast List

| | |
|---|---|
| Chief Constable | |
| Alan Cade . . . . . . . . . . . . . | MARTIN SHAW |
| Deputy Chief Constable | |
| Wes Morton . . . . . . . . . . . | BOSCO HOGAN |
| Detective Superintendent | |
| Rose Penfold . . . . . . . . . . | GILLIAN BEVAN |
| PC Charlie Webb . . . . . . . . | BRIAN BOVELL |
| Diana Lewis . . . . . . . . . . | GILLIAN MARTELL |
| Sam Lester . . . . . . . . . . . | DAVYD HARRIES |
| Andrew Black (HMI) . . . . . | JULIAN GLOVER |
| Nigel Crimmond . . . . | MICHAEL COCHRANE |
| Maria Romero . . . . . . . . | SHELAGH McLEOD |

## Crew List

| | |
|---|---|
| Directors . . . . . . . . . . . . . . | TOM COTTER |
| | RICK STROUD |
| Associate Producer . . . . . . | ELIZABETH HARE |
| Script Editor . . . . . . . . . . . | MAGGIE ALLEN |
| Designer . . . . . . . . . . . . . . | JON PUSEY |
| Art Directors . . . . . . . . . | KIRSTEN DUDLEY |
| | GORDON MEHUISH |
| Make-up . . . . . . . . . . . . . . . | PENNY HUNT |
| Costume Designer . . . . . . . . . . | REG SAMUEL |
| Casting Director . . . . . . . . . . | ANN FIELDEN |